RESEARCH
METHODOLOGY

RESEARCH METHODOLOGY

A HANDBOOK

DR ANANYA MOHAPATRA
Lecturer in Anthropology
Khallikote Autonomous College, Berhampur
Odisha, India

PRADYOT MOHAPATRA
Formerly Senior Research Fellow
Central Institute of Freshwater Aquaculture (CIFA)
Kausalyaganga, Bhubaneswar
Odisha, India

PARTRIDGE
A Penguin Random House Company

To order additional copies of this book, contact
Partridge India
000 800 10062 62
www.partridgepublishing.com/india
orders.india@partridgepublishing.com

CONTENTS

**To the loving memory of our father
Prof. Chandra Sekhar Padaranjan Mohapatra.**

PREFACE

T. N. Madan wrote in 'Research Methodology' (*A Survey of Research in Sociology and Social Anthropology*, vol. 3, ICSSR, 1972) that there are three different meanings of the word *methodology*. The three different meanings respectively are theoretical discussion, techniques of data collection, and data analysis. Hardly any book combines all the three areas. Madan, in the article, attempted a combined treatment of all the three areas.

We often feel that students fail to understand a book or fail to get started with a research work because they are unfamiliar with the methods and techniques of thinking associated with research. The methods and techniques when made explicit allow the student to follow a book or do research. For example, functionalism is better understood if the word *equilibrium* is substituted for it.

Sensing the lacuna, we have attempted to cover in this book the basics of theory, technique, and data. The book is useful to students and researchers of the social sciences and is a supplement to natural scientists. We hope the book would be received well by the academic community.

Chapter I

INTRODUCTION

Anthropologists consider magic as the science of the primitive man. Two principles of magic might be noted.[1] The first one is the law of contiguity. It asserts that by working magic on the pairings of a person's nails or on the clippings of his hair, it is possible to affect the actual man. The second principle, known as the law of sympathy, asserts that like produces like. By working magic on the wax or wooden image of a person, it is possible to affect the real man. The man of science, on the other hand, believes in materialism. He postulates a physical cause (physical connection between cause and effect) behind any effect or effects.

Primitive man was not only a magician; he also was a keen observer of the nature and natural forces around him. The making of the fire and the invention of stone tools must have occurred at an early date. But it was in the field of astronomy that observations were made that later became scientifically useful. 'Having no clocks, they regard instead the face of the sky; the stars serve them for almanacs; they hunt and fish, they sow and reap in correspondence with the recurrent order of celestial appearances.'[2] It was in Egypt, China, and Babylonia that 'from millennial stores of accumulated data, empirical rules were deduced by which the scope of prediction was widened and its accuracy enhanced. But no genuine science of astronomy was founded until the Greeks sublimed experience into theory'.[3] The use of theory meant the data obtained through sense was explained by other means, usually roundabout means. The size and distance of the moon were later calculated by the roundabout way of mathematics rather than by direct eyesight.

Among the Greeks, Thales of Miletus successfully predicted an eclipse of the sun on 28 May 585 BC, Anaximander invented the sundial, and Pythagoras described a twofold motion of earth, round its axis and round the sun. Hipparchus's catalogue of 1,028 stars, completed in 128 BC, proved of help to later astronomers regarding the change of position. The Greek scholars also developed geometry and algebra. Practical activity relating to weights and measures also grew among the Greeks. Geometry developed during the times of Euclid, who used the *reductio ad absurdum* method in the cases of problems and theorems. If a theorem was true, then a chain of consequences were deduced which ended in a conclusion previously known to be true.[4]

Aristotle divided science into many disciplines. Number in arithmetic, magnitude in geometry, stars in astronomy, a man's good in ethics, good of the family in economics, and general good of the state in politics became the standard classification.[5]

Modern science, however, had a late beginning. There were a few pioneers of science, such as Leonardo da Vinci (1452-1519), Nicolaus Copernicus (1473-1543), Francis Bacon (1561-1626), Galileo Galilei (1564-1642), and Isaac Newton (1642-1727), who laid the foundations of the several sciences. Among subsequent scientists, the names of Pierre Simon, marquis de Laplace (1749-1827), James Hutton (1726-1797), Charles Lyell (1797-1875), Charles Darwin (1809-1882), and Gregor Johann Mendel (1822-1884) are important. After that there was a prolific growth in scientific activities, and it appears no use to name all the individual scientists.

Later on science grew mainly through the medium of societies devoted to the publication of scientific research: science became institutionalized. It was no longer possible for the lone scientist to do research at his backyard, unfunded. Science became a subject for the university and research stations.

In earlier years philosophers such as John Stuart Mill used to write extensively on the distinction between science and art.[6] The distinction is even valid today on the ground that art provides the *end*, and science devises means to achieve that end. When in India, the end was self-sufficiency in foodgrain production, agricultural sciences provided the means to achieve such an end: the Green Revolution. Agricultural sciences, plant genetics and extension, shifted the knowledge from the laboratory to the field. Once something is considered scientifically possible, it is subsequently reduced to *rules*. And art consists of these rules. Science then consists of the laws, the principles, and the theories.

A distinction is sometimes made between the pure and the applied sciences. The pure and the applied branches of science respectively are (1) mechanics and the theory of structures, (2) physiology and medicine, (3) economics and business management, and (4) sociology and social work. Note how optimization in economics is applied in poultry management.

> In the most advanced practice, a computer program, containing the nutritional requirements of chickens and the composition of food grains, recomputes the most economic satisfactory mixture of cereal grains, based on daily or even hourly changes in grain prices and directs the mixing machinery accordingly.[7]

The scope of science is delimited by the limited objective pursued by the scientist and facts related to that objective. Science establishes relationship between parts of reality, and therefore, it is abstract. Nevertheless, there are sciences such as physiology that study the abstract part and those such as zoology that study the concrete part. Similarly, while chemistry is abstract, mineralogy is concrete.

The progress of science is attributed to research. There are some conventional rules of research. Maybe it is curiosity that is the starting point of research, but curiosity ought to find a direction to be successful. Maybe there is no fixed recipe for research, and scientists have been illumined by chance happenings in successful research. However, the fortuitous happening occurs to those who are prepared for it. It is the effort of this handbook to make the research worker prepared for any fortuitous happenings.

The special merit of this handbook is that it tries to extract the procedures adopted by real scientists rather than philosophers of science. Nevertheless, it is to be noted that scientists themselves have benefited from the insights of philosophers and admit it publicly. The noted scientist M. Powell at the Le Banquet Nobel 1950 reminds his audience of the famous words of a Greek philosopher:

> Those who are altogether unaccustomed to research are at the first exercise of their intelligence befogged and blinded and quickly desist owing to fatigue and failure of intellectual power, like those who without training attempt a race. But one who is accustomed to investigation, worming his way through and turning in all directions, does not give up the search, I will not say day or night, but his whole life long. He will not rest, but will turn his attention to one thing after another which he considers relevant to the subject under investigation until he arrives at the solution of his problem.[8]

References

1. 'Magic', *Encyclopedia Britannica*, Cambridge: University Press, 1910-11, vol. 17,p.20
2. 'Astronomy', ibid. vol. 2, p. 808.
3. Ibid. p. 808.
4. 'Euclid', ibid. vol. 9, p. 879.
5. 'Aristotle', ibid. vol. 2, p. 517.
6. 'Art', ibid. vol. 2, p. 659.
7. *The Life Sciences*, Washington DC: National Academy of Sciences, 1970, p. 185.
8. M. Powell, Le Banquet Nobel 1950, *Les Prix Nobel en 1950*, 1951, pp. 72-73.

Chapter II

SCIENTIFIC METHOD

Science begins with *observation* and *measurement*. We observe many things: the sky, trees, rivers, and animals. General observation cannot lead to science; observation must be focused. For example, if we are interested in the material culture of a tribe, we should enter the hut of a tribal man and enquire about the artefacts hanging from the roof of his hut. Economists observe the movement in the price of a commodity, whether it be the price of fuel or the exchange rate of the rupee. Early astronomers observed the movement of heavenly bodies before any theory about such movements was proposed. Observation can lead to sound judgment. It sometimes appears that observation, with a little help from paper and pencil, leads to sound prediction. Thus, it is told of a merchant that by keeping records of the movement of prices of a certain commodity for a number of years, he could foretell the rise or fall of the price of that commodity.[1]

Observation of any phenomenon can help build the natural history of that phenomenon. The study of natural history before philosophic interpretation is done can throw light on the origin of objects and events in science. The origin of the earth, of human beings, of plants and animals, and even of social customs has been studied in the past. While the functionalists who are interested in the study of *equilibrium* claim that it is futile to speculate on origin before enough evidence is at hand, it is a historical fact that the study of origin such as the theory of evolution came before time. Greek philosophers had speculated on the fundamental elements from which everything else originated. When the economist Francis Walker said that 'money is what money does', he was trying to shift the focus from the origin of money to what it actually does; he was not concerned with what money *ought* to do or why it originated.

The question of origin, nevertheless, is not a fruitless scientific exercise. It is one of the scientific curiosities inherent in the mind of every scientist. If the forces of nature were as powerful in the past when man did not exist as they today are, then it is not hopeless to reconstruct the past. Geologists surely have advanced the theory of the uniform behaviour of nature whatever the time is.

Before zoology became a science in the strict sense of the word, the so-called zoologists were collectors of specimens. The idea behind the collection of zoological specimens was to keep them in museums. It naturally led to the *classification* of the specimens. The Linnaean binomial terminology with its trinomial refinement into species, subspecies, and varieties established classification as a science in its own right. Classification is crucial to the scientist since ordinary people observe many things without classifying them. They fail to become scientists.

Whether it is the discovery of fire or the discovery of the wheel, some anthropologists are inclined to put forward the view that behind any innovation there was a particular man. The theory so developed is known as historical particularism. We cannot settle the truth of such a view. Modern science has made it clear that once a *clue* to any scientific question is provided by a scientist, teamwork leads to its quick solution.

Religion had provided the *order* to interpret the natural world before science took its place. Order is the essence of science. Though science is orderly, scientific activity does not follow any particular order. The selection of a problem, the collection of data through observation and measurement, the advancement of a hypothesis to explain the data, and the re-examination of the data in terms of the hypothesis—these activities do not follow in the order they are stated here. The sudden flash of genius often helps the scientist to solve his problem. In the case of modern science, it often turns out that to solve any particular problem, several methods are available, and often there is a joint attack by several methods, especially when the matter is statistical.

According to the famous philosopher of science Francis Bacon, the human being is susceptible to many errors or fallacies when he observes anything—the first step of science. In his book *Novum Organum*, Bacon mentioned about four such errors. The first one is *Idola Tribus*, which is common to every human being since he is a member of a tribe or race. We as members of the human race seek order in nature when such order is actually lacking. When we observe anything, we have a tendency to generalize from a few instances, and in the process of generalization of a preconceived idea, we tend to cite affirmative cases while ignoring negative cases. We treat abstractions as real and are helpless against will and passion, which affect our understanding. We try to delve into the ultimate principles of things and consider man as the measure of the universe when man himself is imperfect. The second fallacy, *Idola Specus*, is specific to any individual. We show extreme fondness for either what is ancient or what is modern, and highlight differences and resemblances among things when there is none. The third error, *Idola Fori*, is error of the marketplace. We assign names or words to non-existent things. The fourth error, *Idola Theatri*, pertains to philosophical fallacies. Aristotelian philosophers sought explanation by definition, empirical philosophers drew general conclusions from limited experiments, and superstition introduced poetical or theological notions.[2]

Research has shown that Bacon was opposed to the method of induction by simple enumeration and had instead advocated induction by exclusion or elimination.

We must notice that the basis of induction is comparison. The inductive method is the comparative method, whether the science is social or natural. In the natural sciences, an experimental group is compared with a control group, and conclusion is drawn on the basis of limited evidence. In the social sciences, where no such experiment is possible, the comparison is *before* and *after*, as when the impact of a developmental programme is assessed in a remote tribal area. But the course of history is not shaped *only* by the developmental programme while everything else remained equal, and therefore, it is a kind of pseudo experiment. This problem of 'everything else being equal' has been overcome in our time by the devise of multivariate analysis in statistics.

Before we study about induction, let us see how syllogism in deduction works. Readers are familiar with this example:

> All men are mortals.
> Socrates is a man.
> Therefore, Socrates is mortal.

In the first premise, there is some relationship between men and mortality. In the second premise, there is some relationship between Socrates and his being a man. In the conclusion, the common term between the two premises, *man*, is excluded, and we get the conclusion that Socrates is mortal. There is a relationship between Socrates and mortality. But the truth contained in the conclusion is already contained in the premise such that no new knowledge is achieved. The first premise is not partially verified; it is an axiom, the result of simple experience. A syllogism provides us with knowledge that is certain. The knowledge is not chancy.

We have sketched the notions of induction and deduction. But before scientific activity can begin, there is a need to specify the unit of any particular branch of science. We can, in general, specify 'family' as the unit in social anthropology. But in practice, there are many different types of family, such as the nuclear, the joint, and the extended. Therefore, in any survey, we can specify family as a unit by defining it as father, mother, and their unmarried children. Such a unit would be different from another family where a grandparent lived with the family.

In the physical and the natural sciences, the question of unit takes precedence in research since it is possible to measure anything by several units, and often it is possible to transform any quantity measured in a particular unit into another quantity measured in a different unit. Wealth can be measured in terms of rupees or pounds. Temperature can be measured in degrees Celsius or Fahrenheit.

We have said earlier that will and passion in the Baconian view affected understanding. But understanding is not central to modern science and research. Consider the views of the statistician William F. Ogburn,[3] who says that the tests of knowledge are reliability and accuracy, not understanding. A man might very well understand the wrong explanation that the sun moves around the earth. But that is not knowledge. A man staying in a tribal area for a long time sometimes is considered an expert in their affairs. But professional anthropologists, until recently, had a disdain for such knowledge. It is still a matter of controversy in social anthropology whether to believe such a person or a trained anthropologist who has spent not more than some years' time among the tribes.

The point of Ogburn is that impressionistic knowledge is not to be counted as knowledge since it would not be of 'accurate, systematic, transferable kind called science'.[4] He gives the example of Scandinavians whom an outsider might consider as tall, blue-eyed blonds with long heads and long faces despite the fact that such description fits no more than 15% of the Scandinavian population.

The process of measurement involves two types of error; neither of which has anything to do with the popular meaning of error. *Systematic* error is caused by a defect in the measuring instrument such that every measurement done with the instrument involves the same error. Every time a faulty scale is used to measure length, the same faulty reading persists. This error is minimized with refinement of the measuring instrument. *Random* error is the difference between the true value and the observed value. The difference may either be positive or negative such that, as a whole, they cancel out when sufficient numbers of measurements are taken.

We have said that systematic error persists. The magnitude of the systematic error is *accuracy*. It is either low or high. In the measurement of weekly income, an accuracy of one per thousand is superfluous.

If we have a number of measurements and the arithmetic mean is calculated, it will be largely free from the random error. Let another series of measurement on the object be taken and a second arithmetic mean calculated. The second average will be close to the first. In other words, the average is reproducible. *Precision* is a measure of this reproducibility. In other words, the mean is a reproducible measure.[5]

'The mean of three independent measurements of a quantity may be taken to be three times as reliable as a single measurement and given a weight 3, compared with weight 1 for a single reading.'[6]

Notice that present-day scientists are willing to work with measures, even inaccurate ones, provided that the measure is precise or reproducible. In the measurement of the gross domestic product, we may be far from accurate from the true value, but the fact that it is reproducible and three methods are available for its computation makes it comparable. The gross domestic products calculated by a particular method become comparable over time owing to this reproducibility. Gross domestic products for a number of years can be *deflated* and expressed in real terms such that we can know whether the income level is really increasing or not. The deflated GDP figures are the replicates of each other (the role of money and other confounding variables being discounted), and we can know whether they are really different from each other.

Scientific method does not end with observation and measurement. Imagination is also a part of scientific activity. The canons of induction so carefully formulated by John Stuart Mill are no longer considered ways of discovery, although in the *method of difference*, we have a precursor of the modern experimental method. A hypothesis has become the central part of science, and the method obtained is known as the hypothetico-deductive, or simply the deductive method. S. F. Barker quotes another author, D. C. Williams, in his book as follows: the mode of argument is to rest on the principle that 'if and only if all the consequents of a hypothesis are true, the hypothesis is true, while if all its tested consequents have been proved true, then probably all its consequents are true and so accordingly is the hypothesis'.[7]

Barker writes that hypotheses about atoms, electrons, valence bonds, genes, libidos, and so on will play a vital role as science advances.[8] This is against the verdict of the scientists who long ago believed the electron did not exist or claimed that it did not matter whether the gene was real or fictitious as long as it was there in the chromosome.

The superiority of induction over deduction is known from a long time, M. E. Bennett writes in his book *College and Life*.[9] Bennett's views can be described through the following illustrations. We assume the following:

1. *Result*: Observations as to *weight* in handling different metals
2. *Case*: Each metal handled
3. *Rule*: Characteristics of metals in *general*

The illustration below shows the three scientific methods.

1. Generalizing or induction

   Copper is heavy. (*Case/Result*)
   Iron is heavy. (*Case/Result*)

Therefore, metals are generally heavy. (*Rule*)

2. Explaining or hypothesis

   Metals are generally heavy. (*Rule*)
   Iron is heavy. (*Result*)

Therefore, iron is a metal. (*Hypothesis/Case*)

3. Applying or deduction
   Metals are generally heavy. (*Rule*)
   Aluminium is a metal. (*Case*)
   Therefore, aluminium is heavy. (*Inference/Result*)

In the case of generalizing or induction, we started with the cases and the result and came to the rule. The case was each metal handled, and the result was the weight of each metal handled.

In the case of explaining or hypothesis, we started with the result and the rule and came to the hypothesis in the end. The result was the heaviness of iron, and the rule was the heaviness of metals in general. From this, it was inferred that iron is a metal.

In the case of applying or deduction, we started with the rule and the case, and the result was inferred. The rule was the heaviness of metals, and the case was that of aluminium.

We see here that only in the case of applying or deduction, the inference could be wrong.

We have written the basic procedure involved in induction and deduction. We have also noticed that the inductive method is the method of comparison. We have said that a hypothesis enables us to move from the unknown to the known.

Science is a body of truths, the common principles of which are supposed to be known and separated, so that the individual truths, even though some or all may be clear in themselves, have a guarantee that they could have been discovered and known, either with certainty or with such probability as the subject admits of, by other means than their own evidence.[10]

But before the hypothesis became an integral part of science, the usual procedure was to move from the known to the unknown or from the known to the known. Consider the distinction between *empirical* and *rational* from the field of therapeutics.

A particular condition might have several effects— for example, the condition of gout might manifest itself in itching, pain, cough, or swelling. The physician might try to cure the disease by observing the symptom rather than the condition or cause, in which case the treatment is termed *symptomatic*. Treatment proceeds on the line that similar treatment had worked in the past. But if the treatment fails, the physician is at a loss to explain the cause. This plan of treatment is called *empirical*. In contrast to the empirical treatment is the *rational*, where the cause of the disease is determined. Rational treatment prevents the recurrence of the disease. A particular kind of treatment might have several alternatives that can be used instead. Similarly, other factors affecting the disease might be guarded against. For this, a particular treatment might be *combined* with another or several other for effective result.[11]

The rational procedure in science is working behind several statistical measures such as the analysis of variance, multiple regression, and similar methods such as the discriminant analysis.

Another distinction in science is that between the *synthetic* and the *analytic* method. Nature is synthetic as manifested in the movement of a tide. Past scientists such as Newton and his contemporaries had tried to capture the simplicity of nature in simple equations. But gradually, the procedure of measurement was enlarged with the progress of science and scientific instruments. Measurement of an event was taken at several places, and it was found that the earlier simple equation was overburdened with facts with which it could not bear. Correction became a necessity. The complex whole became the sum of a large number of separate parts, and the method was termed analytic. While particular events were still represented by synthetic equations, the complex whole needed the help of analytic equations.[12]

There is still another method of science known as the method of postulates. Postulates are so general that they are incapable of direct validation. What the scientist does is to derive certain theorems from the postulates. The theorems are so framed that they can be projected against a set of facts. Simple operations such as the agreement or disagreement of the facts with the theorems establish validity or its denial.[13]

It would not be inappropriate to end the chapter with the sociological method of Auguste Comte.[14] This method is based upon observation, experiment, and verification. It differs from the other methods in treating experiment as the observation of *abnormal* social states, and it has a peculiar method of verification. It begins with history or empirical knowledge. Every well-known historical situation is derived from the series of its antecedents. The body of empirical generalizations as to social phenomena thus obtained is compared with the positive theory of human nature. When the empirical generalizations agree with the preparatory conceptions of biological theory, we have *sociological demonstration*. For example, patriotism is said to be demonstrated when it agrees with the biological instinct of territoriality. Nationalism, on the other hand, is an ideology. Many have expressed their doubts over India as a nation since the idea of a nation is a modern one and our territory is defined by many lines, including a line of control.

References

1. 'Applied Mechanics', *The New Popular Educator*, London: Cassell and Company, Limited, no date, vol. 6, p. 35.
2. 'Bacon, Francis', *Encyclopedia Britannica*, Cambridge: University Press, 1910-11, vol. 3, p. 146.
3. William F. Ogburn, 'Statistics and Art', *Journal of the American Statistical Association*, 27 March, 1932, p. 5.
4. Ibid.
5. L. L. Langley, *Cell Function*, New York: Reinhold Publishing Corporation, 1968, pp. 17-18.
6. J. F. Kenney and E. S. Keeping, *Mathematics of Statistics*, New Jersey: D. Van Nostrand Company, Inc., 1954, vol. 1, p. 46.
7. S. F. Barker, *Induction and Hypothesis*, New York: Cornell University Press, 1957, p. 102.
8. Ibid. p. 95.
9. M. E. Bennett, *College and Life*, New York: McGraw-Hill Book Company, 1952, pp. 186-187.
10. 'Sciences', *The Popular Encyclopedia*, London: Blackie and Son, 1897, vol. 12, p. 384.
11. 'Therapeutics', *Encyclopedia Britannica*, op. cit., vol. 26, p. 794.
12. 'Tide', ibid. vol. 26, p. 944.
13. George P. Murdock, *Social Structure*, New York: The Free Press, 1965, p. 127.
14. 'Auguste Comte', *Encyclopedia Britannica*, op. cit., vol. 6, p. 820.

CHAPTER III

HYPOTHESES, THEORY, AND SCIENTIFIC LAW

A hypothesis in science leads us from the unknown to the known. Imagination is necessary to formulate hypotheses in science such as when a palaeontologist reconstructs the past of the earth. But even in routine research that produces routine results, hypotheses have become a part of the process.

There was a law in chemistry that went by the name the *whole number rule*, according to which, the masses of elements as well as the masses of their isotopes could be expressed by means of whole numbers in relation to oxygen. This rule came into prominence when the English physician Prout put forward the hypothesis that 'the atoms of elements are all made up of aggregations of a large or small number of atoms of the lightest known element, hydrogen'.[1]

Prout's hypothesis led to the view that the atomic weights of all elements were exact multiples of that of hydrogen. But later studies found that though the atomic weights of some elements are close multiples of that of hydrogen, there are other elements that defy the rule and exceed the limits of errors associated with observation. There is no whole number rule; fractions are involved, and moreover, the atomic weight of hydrogen itself is not a whole number.

Thus, in the above paragraph, we see that a law can be the ground for further hypothesis, and the hypothesis so formulated might not match the evidence and fails to be accepted. On the other hand, there are hypotheses that have found favour with the scientific community. G. P. Thomson quoted Hermann von Helmholtz on Faraday: 'If we accept the hypothesis that elementary substances are composed of atoms, we cannot well avoid concluding that electricity also is divided into elementary portions which behave like atoms of electricity.'[2] The so-called atoms received the name 'electron' from Johnstone Stoney in 1881 with the correction that it was only electron charge. In 1924, Robert Andrews Millikan commented:

> But the electron itself, which man has measured, as in the case shown in the table, is neither an uncertainty nor an hypothesis. It is a new experimental fact that this generation in which we live has for the first time seen, but which anyone who wills may henceforth see.[3]

A hypothesis sometimes emanates from a theory. In this sense, a theory is equivalent to a definition.

For example, take the definition of beriberi given by Göran Liljestrand.[4] 'Beri-beri shows itself in paralysis accompanied by disturbances in the sensibility and atrophy of the muscles, besides symptoms from heart and blood-vessels, *inter alia,* tiredness and edema.' From the above definition or theory, he hypothesizes that 'a number of circumstances indicated a connection between food and beri-beri; for example, it was suggested that the cause might be traced to bad rice or insufficiency in the food of proteins or fat'. A hypothesis, therefore, is equivalent to a suggestion. Still in other words:

> Although a number of experiments carried out about 50 years ago supported the assumption that, if our food is to have its full value, it must contain something more than the long known basic constituents—protein, fat, carbohydrates, water and salts—yet it is not until our own days that complete certainty has been reached.[5]

Here the hypothesis is equivalent to an assumption. Thus, we see that the synonyms for *hypothesis* are *definition*, *theory*, *suggestion*, and *assumption*.

But sometimes a hypothesis is distinguished from a definition. Sometimes, the scientist 'begins rather with a few simple and familiar experiments and then sets up some definitions which are only descriptions of the experiments and therefore involve no hypothetical elements at all'.[6]

A hypothesis is a declarative statement: there is no difference between the average income of rickshaw pullers of Bhubaneswar and Cuttack. Similarly, when the hypothesis is a definition, it is a case of identity: the word *beriberi* and its definition.

Routine research has formulated many different types of hypothesis; one of which is the distinction between the null and the alternative hypothesis. Examples of null hypotheses are the following:[7]

There is no effect of drug therapy on cholesterol level compared to placebo.

$$H_0: \mu_1 = \mu_2 \text{ or } \mu_1 - \mu_2 = 0$$

Effect of antibiotic on cure rate is 80%.

$$H_0: p_0 = 0.8$$

Average tablet weight for quality control is 300 mg.

$$H_0: W = 300 \text{ mg}$$

The variance of the samples from two procedures is hypothesized to be equal.

$$H_0: \sigma_1^2 = \sigma_2^2$$

Alternative hypotheses are of two types: directional and non-directional. $H_1: \mu_1 \leq 10$ (where the mean is less than 10) is a directional hypothesis while $H_1: \mu_1 \neq \mu_2$ is non-directional. A directional hypothesis requires a one-tailed test, and a non-directional hypothesis requires a two-tailed test.

We have been discussing about theory, hypothesis, and law without making any clear-cut distinctions among the terms. Only philosophers of science, even scientists, often distinguish between the terms, although at other times the terms are used as synonyms. It is in the field of mechanics that the clear manifestation of the term *theory* has come into view.

> The ultimate aim of those who are devoted to any branch of science is to penetrate beyond the phenomena observed on the surface to their ultimate causes, and to reduce the whole complex of observations and empirical rules based upon limited experiences to a simple deductive system of mechanics in which the phenomena observed shall be shown to flow naturally from a few simple laws that underlie the structure of the universe. A correct 'theoria' or physical and logical argumentation deducing from primary laws all the phenomena constitutes the noblest achievement of man in science.[8]

The science of mechanics or rather the theory of mechanics, therefore, does not attempt to study something hopeless such as reality. Without a complete description of reality, mechanics abstracts from reality. Some elements of reality are important than others. These elements are relatively simple and constant. Accidental elements take a back seat, to be incorporated into the analysis later. The process of abstraction leads to simple and definite statements. The more general laws from which the process of deduction begins are subject to modification with the passage of time and the accumulation of evidence. Mathematical legitimacy is sought for the abstract treatment of the subject, but in the end the theory is tested against evidence or fact.[9]

The theory of machines or mechanics had guided other branches of knowledge such as economics in the later part of the nineteenth century. A body of simplified principles, mutually consistent, served the purpose of the neoclassical economists well. This was termed *deduction*, to be distinguished from *induction* when a plethora of particular practices as they are actually found came to the picture.

The theory of mechanics underwent modification with the emergence of the theory of relativity. As P. A. M. Dirac said:

> There exists at the present time a general quantum mechanics which can be used to describe the motion of any kind of particle, no matter what its properties are. The general quantum mechanics, however, is valid only when the particles have small velocities and fails for velocities comparable with the velocity of light, when effects of relativity come in.[10]

Theories, therefore, are revised with the passage of time.

In the past, astronomy and chemistry, similarly, have undergone theoretical modification with the passage of time and the accumulation of new evidence. The notion of 'elements' in chemistry changed its meaning from distinctive qualities to chemical relations. It was later realized that change in the proportion of elements results in the change in substance. In sum, the mathematical idea of ratio and proportions came to play a larger role in chemistry as in many other sciences.[11]

In physiology, vitalism was gradually replaced by materialism.

The chemical discoveries resulting from Wohler's synthesis of urea first showed that typical products of the animal body, the production of which had hitherto been supposed to solely the result of the operation of vital force, could be obtained artificially by purely chemical methods.[12]

In fact, the science of physiology laid the solid foundation for materialism in the life sciences. It has been said that the intermingling of psychological questions with questions of natural science had led to mere confusion of research. Natural science has been called upon to realize its own limits and to confine itself to investigation of the phenomena of the material world.

It is self-evident, however, that only such laws as govern the material world will be found governing material vital phenomena—the laws, that is, which have hitherto been brought to their most exact and most logical development by physics and chemistry, or, more generally speaking, by mechanics. The explanatory principles of vital phenomena must therefore be identical with those of inorganic nature—that is, with the principles of mechanics.[13]

The application of the mathematical principle of linearity to the stretching of muscles in physiology is a testimony to the relevance of mechanical principles in the life sciences.

Thus, we notice that theories formulated a priori are either refuted or accepted on the basis of data or evidence. This is even the position of the institutionalist school in economics. The psychological basis of utility, the capacity to excite desire, seems to have failed, and the reliance on investment and monetary measures attests to the simple fact that an economy is on the move when people get rid of their wealth, when they spend and invest.

Theorization in mechanics and the related sciences has proceeded on two fronts: static models and dynamic models. Static modelling deals with positions of equilibrium, and dynamic modelling involves the incorporation of time into the analysis. Such modellings have necessitated the erection of a 'frame of reference', a prerequisite before theory gets started. The Cartesian coordinate is a simple frame of reference for sciences that have found expression in experienced time and space. The social sciences, especially economics, have made heavy use of the frame of reference. In economics, according to a government economist, it is theorized that had the level of industrial production moved other than it did between period $t - 1$ and period t, then investment in period $t + 1$ would have been different from what it was. This is an example of a dynamic model where 'economic variables occur which relate to different time periods'.[14] The gross domestic product for a particular year, on the other hand, is a static fact. Similarly, if all the economic variables of previous years are treated as *given*, then the model for the next period is considered static.

The word *given* mentioned in the previous paragraph is usually considered the substance of science.

A famous saying of Archimedes brings out this point: '*Give* me a place on which to stand,' said he, 'and I can move the world.' His difficulty was, of course, that there is no such place, unless it be, as he says, 'given'—that is, taken for granted and imagined for the purpose of his discussion.[15]

Now we are in a position to discuss the importance of the concept of *law* in science. The Cambridge economist Alfred Marshall once opined that an economic law is a statement of a tendency. The implication is that the operation of the law is not fully realized in practice. The famous law of demand in economics says that, other things being equal, the price of a commodity and the quantity demanded of that commodity are negatively or inversely related. The law deals with two particulars: price of the commodity and quantity demanded of that commodity. The assumption of other things being equal, or *ceteris paribus*, is invoked to suggest that other things such as the income of the consumer, his taste, and his future expectations about the price of the commodity are *given*. Now, as textbooks suggest, even if the income of a consumer changes, either upward or downward, the law of demand still holds. There is only a shift of the demand curve. But once a consumer is expecting a rise in the price of the commodity in the future, he may expand the demand with the rising price. This, of course, does not mean that the law has failed. The fact is that other things did not remain the same, and once the implication of this is incorporated into the analysis, the deviation from the law is explained. In astronomy, similarly, a wider application for the law of gravitation is sought when it does not operate.

Marshall must have borrowed the idea of law from the gas laws such as that of Robert Boyle. The gas law says, 'When the temperature remains constant, the volume of a given quantity of gas varies inversely as its pressure, that is, the product—Pressure × Volume = Constant.'[16]

At an earlier paragraph, the article says that 'we need to know the pressure, volume, and temperature of a given mass of gas at one time before we are in a position to investigate the changes in *any* [italics added] of these afterwards'.[17]

The point is that a law can have a wider application than its elementary formulation. This is clear from the views of a scientist. A. Tiselius said:

Chemistry became a science only when experiments became systematic and an attempt was made to discuss general laws for the changes in matter. A scientific law should not only render possible a coherent account of all known natural phenomena, but should preferably enable us to predict new ones. When chemists today grope their way forwards in unknown fields, they must always, like the alchemists, try by means of experiments to determine what can and what cannot be done. But they are enormously helped by certain exact general laws which make it possible to predict the result of a chemical reaction under varying external circumstances, for example, different pressures and temperatures. To be able in this way to foresee the result of a chemical reaction is naturally of immense practical value. It is thus often possible nowadays to calculate in advance whether a given chemical process is possible and what conditions favour it. But such laws are also, of course, the basis of any comprehensive picture of the chemical processes in our world, so that research into them has occupied a central position ever since chemistry became a science.[18]

The most important function of a scientific law, therefore, is *prediction*. Even without doing experiments, the scientist can predict the relationship between two or more variables. A scientific law opens before the scientist a world of possibilities and also limitations. Maybe the simple case of inverse proportionality, as illustrated by Boyle's gas law, does not hold in every other case. That is to say all laws cannot be reduced to proportional relations, as the laws of artificial radioactivity demonstrate.

Laws of chemistry are quantitative in nature. Laws in anthropology, such as the law of evolution, are qualitative. The law of evolution says that there is a law-like or fixed relationship between the organisms and their environment so that we could predict the kind of organisms likely to roam in the future, given the environment. Social anthropologists were quick to borrow the idea and expounded the law that the same material environment is likely to generate the same kind of culture. That there was borrowing or give and take, they did not deny. The law as it was formulated only said that, in the absence of borrowing, different cultures would have evolved in the same way, through the same stages.

Many years ago Whitehead expounded the truth, as quoted by G. B. Brown,[19] that the greatest contribution of medievalism to science is 'that every detailed occurrence can be correlated with its antecedents in a perfectly definite manner, exemplifying general principles'. The correlation of an antecedent with its consequent is the basis of law.

There was a time when scientists used to believe that laws of science are immutable. Nowadays it is common knowledge that with the progress of science and the accumulation of evidence, laws also change. Theodore William Richards says:

> The question as to whether or not the supposed constants of physical chemistry are really not constants, but variable within small limits, is of profound interest and of vital importance to the science of chemistry and to natural philosophy in general. If this latter alternative is true, the circumstances accompanying each possible variation must be determined with the utmost precision in order to detect the ultimate reason for its existence.[20]

This suggests that our facts and our laws are statistical in nature.

References

1. H. G. Soderbaum, The Nobel Prize in Chemistry for the year 1922, *Les Prix Nobel en 1921-22*, 1923, p. 86.
2. G. P. Thomson, 'Electronic Waves', ibid., *en 1937*, 1938, pp. 1-2.
3. Robert Andrews Millikan, 'The Electron and the Light-Quant from the Experimental Point of View', ibid., *en 1923*, 1924, p. 6.
4. Göran Liljestrand, The Nobel Prize in Physiology and Medicine for 1929, ibid., *en 1929*, 1930, p. 42.

5. Ibid. p. 45.

6. Robert Andrews Millikan, op. cit., pp. 2-3.

7. Sanford Bolton and Charles Bon, *Pharmaceutical Statistics*, New York: Marcel Dekker, Inc. 2004, p. 107.

8. 'Meteorology', *Encyclopedia Britannica*, Cambridge: University Press, 1910-11, vol. 18, p. 281.

9. 'Mechanics', ibid. vol. 17, p. 955.

10. 'Theory of Electrons and Positrons', P. A. M. Dirac, *Les Prix Nobel en 1933*, 1935, p. 2.

11. 'Chemistry', *Encyclopedia Britannica*, op. cit., vol. 6, p. 33.

12. 'Physiology', ibid. vol. 21, p. 554.

13. Ibid.

14. J. Tinbergen, *Economic Policy: Principles and Design*, Amsterdam: North-Holland Publishing Company, 1967, p. 28.

15. 'Science', *Encyclopedia Britannica*, London: William Benton, 1964, vol. 20, p. 123.

16. 'Pneumatics', *The New Popular Educator*, London: Cassell and Company, no date, vol. 4, p. 307.

17. Ibid.

18. A. Tiselius, The 1949 Nobel Prize for Chemistry, *Les Prix Nobel en 1949*, 1950, p. 30.

19. G. B. Brown, 'The Progress of Physical Science', *Journal of Philosophical Studies*, vol. 5 1930, p. 74.

20. Theodore William Richards, 'Atomic Weights', *Les Prix Nobel en 1914-1918*, 1920, p. 13.

CHAPTER IV

THE DESIGN OF EXPERIMENTS

Experiments in the natural or physical sciences and surveys in the social sciences are a part of the process of research. In the social sciences, where experiment in its strict sense is not possible, a method known as the comparative method is adopted. The comparative method as it has been used by the linguists is admirably summed up by George A. Grierson in his foreword to the book *The Origin and Development of the Bengali Language* (1985 [1926]) by Suniti Kumar Chatterji. Grierson writes:

> There are two possible lines of investigation of this subject. In one, we can follow the example of Beames and view all the forms of speech as a whole, comparing them with each other, and

thence deducing general rules. The other is to follow Trumpp, Hoernle, and Bloch, in taking one particular language as our text, examining it exhaustively, and comparing it with what is known of the others.[1]

Comparison is made even if we make an exhaustive study of a particular language or culture. The name for an exhaustive study of a particular culture is known in social anthropology as ethnography. Comparison to reach general rules, therefore, is known by the name of ethnology. Cross-cultural studies in social anthropology make use of the comparative method, where more than 250 cultures are compared. Before cross-cultural studies were undertaken on a vast scale, the number of cultures compared was limited to around fifty on which the social anthropologist had information. In this endeavour, sometimes the information on a particular culture was restricted to even one research article. The Human Relations Area File of the Yale University made available at the reach of the researcher sitting in a library has vast amounts of information.

In the discipline of economics, where governments all over the world publish regular and vast sums of information on every aspect, the researcher is only required to consult the data. Data on time series is usually obtained from such official statistics. Nevertheless, the economist might make use of cross-section data collected personally by him, such as the data on family budget studies.

One limitation of the comparative method in the social sciences is that the factors affecting the data are nebulous. The experimental scientist compares two situations between which there is agreement in every respect except one. Then, if the two situations differ or have a *real* difference, such difference is attributed to a *controlled* cause. The social scientist, on the other hand, cannot control the affecting factors. The difference between the gross domestic products between two consecutive years might be attributed to increasing productivity or to investment, granted that confounding factors, such as the quantity of money and population growth, are discounted. But still there would be the presence of other confounding factors that cannot be isolated. In a sense, the presence of such confounding factors should not deter the social scientist from reaching the truth or making predictions since the truth is more complex than what we think it is. Secondly, we need not forget the starting point of our study that we had aimed at limited or abstract knowledge, not a complete description of reality. And even in a hard science such as chemistry, many a times an experiment fails, owing to the fact that some ingredient was wet or otherwise. This does not make chemistry in any way inferior.

A failed experiment such as an underground atomic test can nevertheless provide the scientist with valuable data. It is in the story of the history of science that failed experiments provide many clues to a subsequent successful experiment. The scientist whose experiment has failed or whose prediction has not matched reality is not in any way demeaned. He might have provided crucial data to future scientists. It is often stated by writers that the double-helix model of the deoxyribonucleic acid in 1953 by Watson and Crick, which earned them the Nobel Prize, was the result of the accumulation of data and models of previous generations of scientists. What Watson and Crick did was to organize the previous findings and provide a model that matched the facts. This compatibility of every known fact with a model, whether it is done mathematically or physically, is known as *deduction*. This method is germane to the researcher on literature, such as a scholar on drama, who makes an author intelligible by providing an analysis of his works where it is shown that every part agrees with every other part. The whole is intelligible. And it is even the great aim of the physical sciences to present a simple and intelligible picture of the world and the universe such as the law of gravitation or the laws of motion.

The philologist Franz Bopp made a comparative study of many languages where a part (grammatical forms as applied to the verb) was compared with a part. This reinforced the hypothesis of the evolution of the Indo-European languages from a common origin or parentage. This comparison of part with part was later used by the ethnologists in the study of culture. They reduced individual cultures to their elementary parts, such as complexes and traits. Traits from two different cultures were compared to know whether there was a historical connection between the two cultures or whether the two cultures had evolved independently. When many of the traits matched each other, genetic connection was found to be a possibility. (This, however, did not exhaust the possibility of independent evolution.) But there might be one or more traits that are found exclusively in a particular culture and not found in the other. In that case, it was *hypothesized* that the trait absent in the other culture was lost. The same line of argument had been professed by Bopp when he opined to the effect that 'the cognate languages [of Sanskrit such as Persian, Greek, Latin, and German] serve to elucidate grammatical forms lost in Sanskrit'.[2]

What then is the comparative method? Examples cited in the above paragraphs would suggest that we are trying to make science out of historical accidents such as the evolution of languages or cultures. 'Harmonizing words with the actual facts of nature creates history, not science.'[3] But our attempt is something different. Paul Vinogradoff's observation, quoting A. H. Post in the *Encyclopedia Britannica*, can be paraphrased as follows:[4]

> Historical research observes the development of facts of life *within* the range of separate kindreds, tribes, and peoples. Comparative ethnology collects identical facts distributed over vast areas of time and space and draws inferences from these materials to identical or similar causes. It moves from identical or similar effects to identical or similar causes. In the process, new combinations are obtained from the raw data.

The comparative method as substitute for the experimental method is not without its critics. Just observe the address of Harold W. Dodds of Princeton University in 1944 to scientists at a Nobel meeting:

> The method of science utilizes repeated experimentation under controlled laboratory conditions. In large measure the variables with which science deals can be segregated and measured mathematically. Every factor not germane to the

experiment can be and is ignored. But you cannot divide a man. Human nature contains an infinite number of variables, of which at best we can harness only a few at one time. The scholar may select some of them for special treatment but he cannot discard the rest, as science may. When he tries to do so, it is no longer a man that he is studying but a figment of imagination. Our experience with that hoary abstraction, the economic man of classical economics is proof enough of this fact.[5]

A defence against the above criticism is that social scientists have abandoned the study of such a permanent thing as human nature and have concentrated instead upon human behaviour, which can be controlled. In fact, all our coercive laws are aimed at controlling human behaviour through suitable checks and balances. Psychology, sociology, social anthropology, and even economics have for their aim, the control and channelling of human behaviour. We cannot affect behaviour as a whole; a particular behaviour can be influenced. We again aim at the control of a part of human behaviour. If not nature, human behaviour can be abstracted. The concentration on the part to the exclusion of the whole might have affected adversely the growth of not only the social sciences but the natural sciences too. In the practice of medicine, an eye doctor cannot say anything about the ear or nose. But such is the nature of the evolution of science and its methods! Botheration of what is real and what is apparent cannot stop the scientist from his enquiry. When microbiologists expound their doubt on the reality or its absence of an isolated cell under the microscope, we can only say that that should not bother him in the present state of the science. Maybe to unravel the interconnectedness of nature is the task of the future scientist.

After having discussed the use of the comparative method in the social sciences, we are in a position to discuss the role of comparison in the natural and the physical sciences. Sometimes in biology, the scientist makes use of the *historical control.* 'In some cases, an animal may act as its own control if base rates (data on the animal before manipulation) are taken.'[6] A control in this sense is an animal or group of animals which has had no *manipulation.* In sociology, when the impact of an intervention programme on the life of a group of people is studied, the condition of the people before the intervention serves as the historical control. Then the difference seen in the life of the people might be attributed to the intervention. This design is sometimes called the *before-after* design.

In contrast to the above design, there is the *after-only* design. Here the two groups for comparison are selected before the manipulation is introduced on the experimental group. Then the scientist tries to know whether the manipulation had any *real* effect on the experimental group or the difference observed was only apparent.

In both of the above experimental situations, we are trying to determine the *change* observed after the manipulation. An experiment, therefore, is carried out to measure the extent of the change. Whether it is the change in demand after a change in income or the change in national income after a change in the magnitude of investment, we are in the world of science. In economics and some other sciences, we may have to content ourselves with the fact that we can only speak of the *direction* of the change and not its *magnitude*.

In comparative anatomy, a scientist is sometimes able to reconstruct a whole animal from the fragments of its parts. In biblical studies, we have the *fragment hypothesis*, where a part of the available literature is used to reconstruct the whole story. Modern sampling, similarly, is a fragment or part used to draw inference on the whole. These are valid scientific methods and have been rewarding in the past.

Experiments are not possible in astronomy; it is also not possible in economics. However, in geology some limited forms of experiments are possible. The geologist, first of all, is an observer. He observes the rocks, the mountains, the seas, and other natural formations. He discovers fossils of sea animals on the land and hypothesizes that such lands were under sea once upon a time. He possibly cannot go very deep into the earth, and, therefore, simulates the temperature and other factors in a laboratory to observe their impact upon rocks and other natural elements.

In medical science, the design of experiments has reached its logical perfection. Medical science is intermediate between the hard sciences, such as physics and chemistry, where the experimental object is inanimate and the errors associated with the experiment are confined to the experimenter and the instruments, and the social sciences, where the object of the experiment is the human being or his groupings. The classic *randomized controlled trial* in therapeutics 'demands *equivalent groups* of patients *concurrently treated* in different ways'.[7] Equivalence demands equivalence regarding age, sex, race, duration of disease, severity of disease, and others. Equivalence is obtained through random allocation of patients. Random allocation is preferred over alternate allocation to the two groups. Concurrent treatment is required to take care of the conditions regarding the disease, such as severity with time, virulence, and the weather. The conditions for both the treatment and the experimental group ought to remain similar.

In contrast to the randomized controlled trial, there is the technique of *double blind*, where the patient does not know what treatment he is receiving and the doctor also does not know what he is giving, whether the drug or the placebo.

Not only in medicine but also in agriculture too that experimental designs are possible, such as the *uniformity trial*. A field consisting of 500 plots can be treated in the same way to know whether there is any natural advantage to any of the sides since it is known that fertility varies across the plots. The distance between the successive plots is the *limitation* of the design; it has nothing to do with statistics. The uniformity trial experiment can be converted to the randomized block design with the help of some additional techniques.

References

1. George A. Grierson, 'Foreword', in S. K. Chatterji, *The Origin and Development of the Bengali Language*, New Delhi: Rupa and Co., 1985 [1926], p. v.
2. 'Bopp, Franz', *Encyclopedia Britannica*, Cambridge: University Press, 1910-11, vol. 4, p. 241.

3. 'Scaliger', ibid. vol. 24, p. 284.

4. 'Jurisprudence, Comparative', *Encyclopedia Britannica*, op. cit., vol. 15, p. 583.

5. Address of President Harold W. Dodds of Princeton University, *Les Prix Nobel en 1940-1944*, 1946, p. 65.

6. Richard A. Boolootian and Karl A. Stiles, *College Zoology*, New York: Macmillan Publishing Co., Inc., 1976, p. 2.

7. D. R. Laurence and P. N. Bennett, *Clinical Pharmacology*, Edinburgh: Churchill Livingstone, 1980, pp. 70-71.

CHAPTER V

THE SOCIAL SCIENCES

Are experiments in the social sciences possible in the manner in which they are possible in chemistry and biology? It has been said that William Harvey demonstrated the circulation of blood through experiments. He demonstrated it through three methods into which we need not go here. The application of more than one method to demonstrate any phenomena is the hallmark of science. As Dr Harold Jeffreys says in an authoritative article on the scientific method, 'We can recognize a table by sight without touching it, or by touch in the dark. But it is more conclusive to have both data.'[1] In the same paragraph, Jeffreys goes on to say that the discovery of Neptune was certified by two methods, gravitational theory and observation. The gravitational theory gave the correct mass of the planet, the visual determination, the position. But science does not stop with a unique event. It leads from observations to the generalization of such observations such that prediction is possible. But in the process of the repeated observation of anything, knowledge and experience has a premium over youth. Statisticians ask the question, 'How would the physician Millikan have measured it?' As the cardiologist John Neff says in an article, 'A student who hears rales in a patient that the attending physician also hears is said to be *accurate* [italics added].'[2] But accuracy only is not sufficient. *Precision* is also needed. To quote Neff again, 'If a blindfolded examiner hears faint rales nine out of ten times in the same patient, he is precise.' Here Neff is concerned with counting, and counting is said to be more exact than measurement.

The social sciences are somewhat lagging behind the natural sciences on the question of measurement. Economics is somewhat better placed compared to the other social sciences. Value or price can measure human motive well than any other conception. There is the famous law of diminishing utility that says that as we have more of anything, our desire for any more of it diminishes. But this is only possible when the initial units of anything are more valuable than the terminal units. Economists avoid this difficulty by saying that value is determined at the marginal unit, not prior to it.

The economist still manages his difficulties more smartly than a psychologist. He has the device of *ceteris paribus*, or other things being equal. The effect of the other factors affecting demand can be brought about in short steps, one by one, to examine their effect on the demand for anything. The other factors affecting demand too are quantitative, such as income and the prices of other goods. However, even with these added advantages, it cannot be said that the economist is placed at ease compared to a fishery scientist, who can measure the growth rate of fish in a pond.

Sociology and anthropology are the sister disciplines that share some of the research methods and techniques. Anthropology in the last century grew in opposition to the doctrine of social evolution that was characteristic of the nineteenth century. Functionalism, or the synchronic study of culture, was an early-twentieth-century addition. As Julian H. Steward says in *Theory of Culture Change*, 'In some instances, there are constellations of phenomena which occur repeatedly because certain phenomena presuppose others.'[3] These regularities are synchronic. Steward goes on to say in the same paragraph, 'In other cases, there is a succession of similar constellations which succeed one another in a regular and predetermined way because of developmental laws.' These developmental regularities are diachronic.

Not only the distinction between synchronic and diachronic, which is central to anthropological research and is reminded by university professors to their students, the distinction between phonetic and phonemic sometimes emerge important in the distinction between the *etic* and the *emic* approach. These terms are from linguistics. As George A. Miller of the Massachusetts Institute of Technology says, 'For linguistic purposes the phonemes replaced the highly variable sounds that occur in actual speech. Thus a talker might produce a great hodge-podge of vocal symbols, but the symbols he was trying to produce were really the phonemes.'[4] Thus began the distinction between *phonetics* and *phonemics*.

What we have been learning from the above paragraphs is the repeatability or regularity of any phenomena. Sometimes the very regularity of any phenomena is important; it shows the reproducibility of any phenomena. Sometimes the accidental is explained by its reference to the principle, as explained in the distinction between phonemics and phonetics.

The methods and techniques of social research go beyond what we have sketched above, and in particular, we can mention a few. Before a research scholar goes to field, he ought to have found a control group for his experiment. Suppose he is interested to learn the academic standard of tribal students studying in Bhubaneswar; then for his *control*, he should have the record of tribal students studying in a residential school in some remote tribal area. The experimental variable here is the change of atmosphere associated with living in a modern city such as Bhubaneswar.

Anthony H. Richmond, who has written the article 'Social Scientists in Action', [5] has mentioned a number of techniques. In content analysis, the *ratio* of the favourable to unfavourable responses on any topic (such as race) could be plotted for a number of years to know the public opinion. Random sampling is appropriate whenever we wish to have opinion of a cross section of the population. Participant observation is effective when the researcher surreptitiously begins to mix with the people he wanted to investigate. Guided interview asks carefully formulated questions that can be *coded* at the stage of data analysis. Unguided or open-ended interview helps to elicit information that would not have come to surface in a guided one by providing flexibility in the answer. Accumulation of observations and interviews over a period is known as cumulative interview. Life history throws light on the past history; this helps to understand the present situation. Field notes too are important. Richmond says that unemployment and poverty issues of coloured people were the favourites of social surveys in Britain.

Economists and statisticians in the past have made use of a multiplicity of sampling techniques, such as random sample, selected random sample, stratified sample, and controlled sample. Thus, in consumer purchases studies, it has been possible to hold other things constant. The study of changes in expenditure pattern with increase in income has been made possible while holding occupation and family type constant.

Sociologists have made great use of correlation. A drawback of correlation is that we might have correlation between two variables, but that might be owing to the effect of an, as yet, undisclosed variable.

The use of sampling and other statistical techniques is growing in the social sciences. The fundamental principle behind sampling perhaps is that it is not the *proportional* size of the sample but the *absolute* size of the sample that is relevant. There are many ways of stating this principle, and we would state some of the ways. In fact, there is a trade-off between sampling error (accuracy) and the size of the sample. But once the sample has reached a certain size, its accuracy settles around a steady value, and thereafter, there is no point in increasing the sample size. Thus, for a given level of accuracy, the sample size can be calculated and vice versa. Even in public opinion surveys, therefore, a sample of 1,500 to 2,000 becomes adequate.

Students of social science often fail to understand the concept of significance. There are statistical tables to find out whether a difference between two means is significant. However, there are certain intuitive ideas that can help the student. Thus as Harold Jeffreys[6] says in the context of a genetical problem, when we expect a probability of ¼ in a particular problem and get 20 to 30 cases out of 100, our result might not be significant. But if we get 50 or 10 out of 100 cases, then the result is likely to be significant. In other words, the result is improbable or is not explained by chance.

Similarly, when we are calculating the standard error of a difference between two means, we can calculate a t. Here t is equivalent to the obtained difference divided by the standard error of the difference of the mean. When the obtained difference is three or more times the standard error of the difference, it is considered significant. In other words, the sample suggests that the populations from which they have been derived are different.

Similar intuitive ideas are found in the chi-square test. According to Jeffreys, the chi-square as introduced by Pearson is

$$\chi^2 = \frac{(x + y + x' + y')(xy' - x'y)^2}{(x + y)(x + x')(x' + y')(y + y')}.$$

Jeffreys says:

There is strong evidence for the existence of a difference if chi square is more than 8; if it is less than 3 and the smallest of the four factors in the denominator is more than about 100 there is strong evidence that any difference between the sampling ratios represents nothing but the ordinary uncertainty of sampling.[7]

It should be noted that while chi-square tests the significance of difference of frequencies within classes, the *t*-test tests the significance of difference between means.

In contrast to the above, multivariate analysis is used when there is more than one controlling factor affecting the dependent variable, when there is relationship between the factors, when the factors are ranked in importance, and when the intervention of one factor reinforces or damps down the effect of another.[8]

In regression analysis, we want to know how much of the total variation in the dependent variable can be attributed to chance and how much to the relationship between the dependent and the independent variable. The total deviation of the dependent variable from the mean of the dependent variable can be divided into two parts: (1) the difference between the regression line and the mean value and (2) the difference between the observed value of the dependent variable and the regression line. In other words, the total deviation of the observed value of the dependent variable from the mean consists of the above two parts.

References

1. Harold Jeffreys, 'Scientific Method and Philosophy', *Science News 3*, Penguin Books Ltd., 1947, p. 79.
2. John Neff, 'The Value of Diagnostic Tests: Probability Considerations in Clinical Medicine', *Diagnostic Procedures*

in Cardiology: A Clinician's Guide, eds. James V. Warren and Richard P. Lewis, Chicago: Year Book Medical Publishers Inc., 1985, p. 17.

3. Julian H. Steward, *Theory of Culture Change*, Urbana: University of Illinois Press, 1973, p. 4.

4. George A. Miller, 'Psycholinguistics', *Handbook of Social Psychology*, ed. Gardner Lindzey, Reading: Addison-Wesley Publishing Company, Inc., 1954, vol. 2, p. 695.

5. Anthony H. Richmond, 'Social Scientists in Action', *Science News 27*, Penguin Books Ltd., 1953, pp. 69-92.

6. Harold Jeffreys, op. cit., p. 71.

7. Ibid. p. 72.

8. Richard J. Chorley and Peter Haggett, eds., *Frontiers in Geographical Teaching*, London: Methuen and Co. Ltd, 1970, p. 159.

CHAPTER VI

THE ROLE OF STATISTICS IN EXPERIMENTS

There is a misconception that statistics plays a primary role in the design of experiments. Statistics and the statistician do play a role, but equally, the choice of the experiment by the scientist is crucial. Thomas Hunt Morgan, who added two more rules to Mendelian genetics, is praised for the design of his experiment. On the occasion of the Nobel Prize in Physiology or Medicine for 1933, Folke Henschen of the Caroline Institute said:

Another cause for Morgan's success is no doubt to be found in the ingenious choice of object for his experiments. From the beginning Morgan chose the so-called bananafly, Drosophila melanogaster, which has proved superior to all other genetic objects known so far. This animal can easily be kept alive in laboratories, it can well endure the experiments that must be made. It propagates all the year round without intervals. Thus a new generation can be had about every twelfth day or at least 30 generations a year. The female lays about 1,000 eggs, males and females can easily be distinguished from each other, and the number of chromosomes in this animal is only 4. This fortunate choice made it possible to Morgan to overtake other prominent genetical scientists, who had begun earlier but employed plants or less suitable animals as experimental objects.[1]

The address, however, later added that Morgan had arrived at the truth of exchange of genes as a real exchange of parts between the chromosomes by statistical analysis rather than by direct examination of the chromosomes. This abstract way of thinking corresponds to a stereometric reality.[2]

The deductive power of statistics is evident from the above paragraph. The introductory part of statistics begins with descriptive statistics, such as the calculation of an average and dispersion. The descriptive part thereafter is supplemented to the inferential part; the inferential part plays the major role in science through the idea of probability.

But before we introduce ourselves to theoretical statistics, we need to know upon what kind of data the procedures and formulas of statistics can be applied.[3] We can, for example, distinguish our data as male and female. We can, for example, classify the voters registered in a village having a preference for different political parties. The voters, politically, are simply different. We can, in classifying a population, label males as 1 and females as 2. But the assignment of such numerical values does not imply that females are *twice* better off in any characteristic than males. Such classification or naming is known as a *nominal* scale.

Another scale of classification is the *ordinal* scale. Students coming in an examination as first, second, third, and so on constitute an ordinal scale. A man expressing his preference for tea over coffee and other beverages is making use of an ordinal scale. He possibly cannot say how much he prefers tea to coffee in the sense that the cost of a pen is thrice the cost of a pencil. The ordinal scale is used in economics to order preference. If in any situation involving choice, *A* is preferred to *B* and *B* is preferred to *C*, then *A* is preferred to *C*. The rationale behind such ordering is to move to a unique position given the alternatives. When many people express preference for tea over coffee, we say that tea is the mode or fashion.

An *interval* scale is superior to the above two scales in the sense that here the intervals upon the scale count for *equal* differences. But this scale lacks a true zero point. A person scoring zero in a test does not lead to the absurdity that his intelligence was zero. There is no such thing as zero temperature. Since the scale lacks a true zero point, we cannot say that 40° centigrade is *twice* hotter than 20° centigrade, although we can say that it was so many equal degrees hotter or 20° hotter.

A *ratio* scale has a true zero point. Here we can say something is *twice* or *thrice* than something else. When rainfall is 10 millimetres, it is twice the rainfall of 5 millimetres. When rain did not fall, the scale registered a zero, the total absence of rain. Kilogram, litre, income, and other such measures are of the ratio type.

The nominal and the ordinal scale do not have any unit or units attached to them. The science of mechanics and the other somewhat hard sciences following the lead of mechanics have used many different types of units for the purpose of measurement. When it is possible to measure something or express something in a unit different from the original unit in which it had been measured, we say that *absolute measurement* is possible. The science of mechanics is full of all such measurements into which we need not go here. We can say:

> In physical science the uniformities in the course of phenomena are elucidated by the discovery of permanent or intrinsic relations between the measurable properties of material systems. Each such relation is expressible as an equation connecting the numerical values of entities belonging to the system. Such an equation, representing as it does a relation between actual things, must remain true when the measurements are referred to a new set of fundamental units.[4]

Later, the method of not only traditional mechanics but the newer mechanics such as the behaviour of atoms was applied to other fields. In the words of P. A. M. Dirac:

> There is in my opinion a great similarity between the problems provided by the mysterious behaviour of the atom and those provided by the present

economic paradoxes confronting the world. In both cases one is given a great many facts which are expressible with numbers, and one has to find the underlying principles. The methods of theoretical physics should be applicable to all those branches of thought in which the essential features are expressible with numbers.[5]

The same line of argument was later advocated by M. Bertil Lindblad. While speaking in the honour of Fermi, he said:

You are one of those who have taught us to appreciate the greatness of subtle things. The interior of the atomic nuclei is certainly a very small world. And yet it exhibits in its small sphere, as in a nut-shell, the essential properties of matter and the fundamental laws of nature.[6]

We do not claim to know how far the methods of mechanics can be applied to the life and the social sciences. Indeed, it is the claim of a physician, John Neff, that 'there are conflicting test results, which is inevitable when we measure anything by different methods'.[7]

Our purpose behind the above few paragraphs was to look for something that can qualify as the fundamental quantities in statistics. Do the mean, the median, and the mode qualify for that purpose? Mode is sometimes expressed in terms of the median and the mean, and in the normal distribution, the three measures coincide. Given the mean and the standard deviation, itself a super mean, the normal distribution is at our service to make a difference to the world of the scientist from the mundane world.

The arithmetic mean, or simply the mean, is calculated by summing a number of *like* quantities and then dividing the summation by the number of items or observations. The arithmetic mean calculated for a *population* or universe is called a *parameter*; the arithmetic mean calculated for a *sample* of values is called a *statistic*. The number of observations for a population is denoted by N; the number of observations for a sample is denoted by n. The formula for arithmetic mean for a sample of values is given by

$$\bar{x} = \frac{\sum x}{n}.$$

Here the notation $\sum$ stands for the Greek upper-case letter sigma: it instructs us to sum all the x values under our consideration. The x values can be the weight of a particular cell taken for a number of times or the measurement of the length of a table taken for a number of times. The calculation of the mean of such values enables us to determine the most representative value than any observed value. In fact, the mean may not coincide with any of the observed values. When a number of measurements of the same quantity are taken, there are either positive or negative deviations from the true value. In the process of the calculation of the mean, the positive and negative deviations from the true value tend to be cancelled, and we are nearer to the true value.

In some studies such as the level of income of a group of individuals, the values are different in the sense that we are not measuring any particular income time and again. Rather, we are measuring income of a group of people belonging preferably to a class such as daily-income earners. The idea is to reach a representative income that can direct action. If in the category of daily-income earners, we mix the income of some speculators on the stock exchange, the mean income would be far from representative. The calculation of the arithmetic mean would still be sound from the mathematical point of view, but it would not serve any purpose. A millionaire is balanced by several paupers, but such balancing would have no purpose. A millionaire is *unlike*, or different from, a pauper.[8]

When the number of observations under consideration is large, it is appropriate to group the data before the arithmetic mean is calculated. Some information/accuracy is lost in the process of grouping. The arithmetic mean calculated by a computer would be different from hand calculation (after grouping) since the computer makes its calculation directly upon the observations.

One elementary procedure of grouping is to define the class interval. For example, let the class interval be 96-100. Let the number of observations under this group be 5 and the numbers be 96, 96, 97, 98, and 100. Then the frequency (f) of numbers is 5. In the calculation of the arithmetic mean, what we do is to take the midpoint of the class interval 96-100, that is 98, and then multiply it by the frequency 5. If the frequency is denoted by f and the midpoint by x, then the formula for arithmetic mean of grouped data is

$$\overline{x} = \frac{\sum fx}{n}.$$

A mathematical characteristic of arithmetic mean is that the addition of any numerical quantity (positive or negative) to each of the measurements produces the addition of the same quantity to the average, so that the calculation may often be simplified by taking some particular measurement as a new zero from which to measure.[9]

Textbooks on statistics call the above method of calculation the shortcut method. For example, for grouped or continuous series data, the shortcut method is

$$\overline{x} = A + \frac{\sum fd}{n}.$$

In the above equation, A stands for the assumed mean that is selected from the midpoint values of the variable. The symbol d stands for m—A, or the difference between the midpoint values and the assumed mean.[10]

The second measure of central tendency is the median. The median also is a kind of balance, but here a millionaire is balanced by a pauper. It is not affected by extreme items since if we change a value from 200 to 2,000 at one extreme, with the order of the numbers remaining the same, the median is unaffected. If the number of observations is odd, say 11, the median is the value at the sixth position. If the number of observations is even, say 10, strictly speaking, there is no median. The convention here is to take the fifth and the sixth positional values and calculate their mean value.

For grouped data or the continuous series, the median is calculated by the following formula:

$$L + \frac{\frac{n}{2} - c.f.}{f} \times i$$

Here in the above formula, L is the lower limit of the median class. The symbol n stands for the number of observations and f for frequency of the median class. The symbol $c.f.$ stands for cumulative frequency of the class preceding the median class, and i is the class interval of the median class.

The idea of point of balance is given up in the calculation of the mode. There might be observations for which there are two modes (bimodal) or more than two modes (multimodal). When we are studying a homogeneous population such as a tribal village, the modal class is the typical class. Any characteristic of the village is reflected through the modal class. When the variability in the population increases, the mode loses its appeal to the statistician. The mode is useful in determining the demand for the most used size of shoes or shirts, and this helps the producer, the retailer, and the consumer. There are occasions when the frequency of an event increases suddenly. The demand for textbooks goes up after students take admission into colleges. A typical month, therefore, appears as the modal month in the purchase of textbooks. If there are *two* months in a year when taxes can be paid, we have a bimodal case.

Mode is defined as the difference between three median and two mean. And this suggests that even when the mode is ill-defined (it is either bimodal or multimodal), there is a specific relationship among the three measures: mean, median, and mode. In other words, there is some scope for to derive one measure of central tendency from the other two.

Many a time, any measure of central tendency is insufficient to convey the typical information about a distribution. The arithmetic mean of 75, 75, and 75 is 75; the arithmetic mean of 50, 75, and 100 is also 75. But the variability of the two series of values is different. It is usually required to calculate the variability or dispersion of a sample of values around the central tendency, and the tendency selected for this purpose is the arithmetic mean since it only has certain mathematical properties.

In many experiments in biology, there occurs a deviation of observations from some expected or theoretically expected ratio.[11] Let us imagine that the students of the biology department of a university are doing an experiment where the expected ratio (expected on the average) is 3:1. On the average, we are expecting 3 normal for 1 mutant. Then, if the sample size of a student is 400, we are expecting a ratio 300:100. But there are inherent limitations to any experiment. Since the experiment is based upon a sample, there is the chance for sampling error. With the above consideration included, we might observe the observed ratios to depart from the expected ratio, and this departure can be expressed in terms of percentage. For now, let us consider the absolute departure from the normal for every student. Some students might have more than

300 normal and some less than 300. When we add all the deviations from the normal disregarding sign and divide the total by the number of students, we get the average, or *mean absolute deviation.*

We have said above that in an experiment in biology, the mean absolute deviation is calculated from deviations from an expected ratio. When there is no such theoretical or expected ratio such as in the social sciences, the mean absolute deviation can still be calculated from the mean. In fact, the expected ratio in the biological experiment was the expected ratio on the *average*, or the mean. The formula for the mean absolute deviation is

$$MAD = \frac{\sum \left| x - \overline{x} \right|}{N}.$$

An important point to note is that if we take the deviation from the median instead of the mean, the numerator in the above formula shall be the minimum.[12] Secondly, when there are occasional large deviations in the observations, the mean absolute deviation is applied.

In the above example, when we dealt with a 3:1 ratio, the distribution of observations was binomial, much like a coin-tossing experiment, where the outcome is either head or tail. The mean absolute deviation measured the *error* of the ratio from the expected 3:1 ratio. With the calculation of the mean absolute deviation, we have got the error of this particular experiment. But with another step added, we can calculate the general nature of the error. In other words, we can make use of inferential statistics in reaching a generalization regarding the error of the ratio. We can say whether the error was simply due to sampling error; in other words, whether the error was likely to arise in another sample of the same size. In other words, when we moved from the *data* to the *result*, we need to specify whether the result was significant (improbable) or due to mere chance (probable).

To do this, we need to calculate the *standard error*. The word *standard* suggests that some arbitrary standard is being defined, such as a kilogram. In this example, the ratio 3:1 is written as a proportion such as 0.75:0.25. Then, the proportion is multiplied: 0.75 × 0.25. The result of the multiplication is divided by the sample size, and then the square root is taken. Thus, we have the square root of (0.75 × 0.25) / 400 = 0.022. The general formula for the standard error of a ratio, *p:q*, is

$$SE_r = \sqrt{\frac{pq}{n}} \, .$$

We have calculated the standard error of the ratio 3:1 as 0.022. In any particular experiment, we have got a deviation of 3% (0.03) from our expected ratio of 3:1. We now divide this deviation by the standard error. We have 0.03 / 0.022. The quotient is 1.4. The deviation, therefore, is 1.4 times the standard error. Is the deviation significant and *unlikely* to arise in another sample of the same size? Books on statistics tell us that in this particular case, the chances of getting a deviation

1.4 times the standard error is 1 in 6. This is not considered significant. Such a deviation is likely to arise by chance. Had the chances of getting a deviation as great as the deviation in question been 1 in 20 or less, it would have been considered significant. Thus, when the probability of the deviation is less, we are considering it significant. When the probability of the deviation is more, we do not consider it significant.

Instead of operating with the mean absolute deviation of a ratio, we could have used the standard deviation. The standard deviation of a binomial distribution is given by

$$\sigma = \sqrt{pqN} \cdot$$

Thus, we would have calculated the square root of $0.75 \times 0.25 \times 400$. And then we would have divided the result of this value by the percentage of deviation: 3. The result would have been called the u value. In this particular example, we would have got a value of 0.34—that is, 0.34 standard deviations. Next, we consult a table of u values and find that when u is 0.3, the probability associated with it is 0.764. Since 0.764 is greater than 0.05, or 5%, we accept the null hypothesis that the ratio is 3:1. The result is not significant. Note that the table for u values is obtained from normal distributions.

We could continue our discussion of the binomial distribution and consider cases when we have enumeration or count data *within* a class that can have *more* than two values. Instead of two values, we could have a ratio 9:3:3:1. In this case, the chi-square test is the appropriate test. It is given by the formula

$$\chi^2 = \sum \left(\frac{d^2}{e} \right).$$

Here d stands for the difference between the observed and expected values; e represents the expected value. Division is performed *before* summation.

We could have used the chi-square test in the example where we have used the u test. And had we done so, we would have got a result that was not significant.

Thus far, we have been dealing with enumeration or count data. We could have most of the time at our disposal measured data. Here, the role of the standard deviation becomes paramount. Data on height is measured data on which the standard deviation is easily applied.

Statisticians prefer to use the *standard deviation* in place of the mean absolute deviation for its mathematical properties. For example, in the experiment in biology described above, we took the absolute values of deviations from the mean disregarding signs. We could have taken the deviations from the mean and then squared it and used another formula such as one given below:

$$\sigma^2 = \frac{\sum (x - \mu)^2}{N}$$

The above is the formula for the population *variance* since it includes the population mean (μ) and the population itself (N). When deviations are squared from the population mean, there is no negative value. And the summation is a positive number. But statisticians go further and calculate the square root of the variance, or σ^2, and call it the standard deviation, or σ. There are certain statistical reasons behind squaring the deviations and then taking the square root, and statisticians consider it good practice. In the process of calculation, large deviations are overemphasized, or in other words, the weight of the large deviations increases.

The population mean (μ) and the size of the population (N) are usually not known. Therefore, they are calculated from a sample, and accordingly, there is some change in the formula for the sample variance and the sample standard deviation. The sample variance is given by the formula

$$s^2 = \frac{\sum (x - \bar{x})^2}{n}.$$

The above formula for the variance of the sample has a tendency to underestimate the variance. We have, in the process of the calculation of the sample mean, used one number of degrees of freedom.

The concept of degrees of freedom is difficult to understand.[13] One simple example of it is to calculate the mean of a set of values, for example, of 4, 6, and 2. The mean of the above three numbers is 12 / 3 = 4. Now let us put x in the place of the last value in the series 2. Then we have $(4 + 6 + x) / 3 = 4$. Then, x can take the only value of 2, no other value. In other words, we have used up one degree of freedom in the calculation of the arithmetic mean. This situation arises since the deviations from the arithmetic mean equal zero.[14]

$$\sum (x - \bar{x}) = 0$$

In other words, there is a linear connection linking the x's with the mean.

The formula for the sample variance therefore is given by

$$s^2 = \frac{\sum (x - \bar{x})^2}{n - 1}.$$

Here in the denominator, we have not taken the size of the sample, n, but the *degrees of freedom, n – 1.*

The square root of the variance is the *standard deviation*. Standard deviation is usually larger than the mean absolute deviation. It is given by the formula

$$s = \sqrt{\frac{\sum (x - \bar{x})^2}{n - 1}}.$$

The variance was given in squared units of the original observations; the standard deviation, since it is the square root of the variance, is in the original units as the observations are.

The standard deviation has many useful mathematical properties. Each time we draw a sample from the same population, we are likely to get a mean different from the earlier one. Theoretically, we can have a distribution of sample means. Even if the parent distribution is not normal, the distribution of sample means is likely to be normal. The way we calculated the standard error of a ratio, we can calculate the standard error of a mean. It is given by the formula

$$SE_m = \frac{\sigma}{\sqrt{n}} \cdot$$

In practice, we have only *one* sample, and the sample mean is calculated. Then we calculate (sample mean ± standard error). The meaning of this calculation is that if we got a large number of samples of a particular size, then about 2/3 of the means of these samples would probably be included between the range defined by our sample mean ± standard error.

When we have calculated the standard error of the mean, we can compare whether our sample mean is representative of the true or population mean. For this, there is something called the *t* statistic. The *t* statistic is a versatile one, and there are several uses of it. However, the original use of the *t* statistic was confined to know (1) whether a sample mean is representative of the population mean and (2) whether there is any significant difference between the means of two samples.

The *t* statistic had originally been developed for small samples. It assumes a normal distribution. The question is whether the sample can be regarded as drawn from a normal universe with a prescribed mean when the standard deviation (s) is *estimated* from the sample. From the distribution of s and $\bar{x}$, Student proceeded to the distribution of the ratio $z = \dfrac{\bar{x}}{s}$ and thereby gave us a new probability curve as Rietz has said. In earlier times, the ratio of $\bar{x}$ to s or some multiple of s was required to enter a normal probability table for the purpose of statistical significance. Now, instead of using $z = \dfrac{\bar{x}}{s}$, we are using

$$t = \frac{\bar{x}}{s_{\bar{x}}}$$

$$\text{where } s_{\bar{x}} = \frac{s}{\sqrt{n-1}}$$

is the standard deviation of $\bar{x}$.

The use of the t statistic in statistics illustrates the principle of feedback. The statistician is the governor who controls, say, the weight of tablets. Let the average weight of tablets at the prescribed level be 300 mg. Then, when the obtained average weight departs significantly from the prescribed weight, the statistician smells something is wrong and advises precaution.

The t statistic is also useful to compare two sample means for testing the significance of the differences of two means. It is assumed that the parent distributions are normal.

When there are several factors, it is not advisable to make a series of *t*-tests, taking two factors at any time. If we did so, the errors associated with the process go on increasing, and no useful result is obtained. In such a situation, it is desirable to make an analysis of variance.

References

1. Folke Henschen, The Nobel Prize for Physiology and Medicine for the year 1933, *Les Prix Nobel en 1933*, 1935, p. 58.

2. Ibid. p. 59.

3. Charles G. Morris, *Psychology*, New Jersey: Prentice-Hall, Inc., 1976, pp. 595-597.

4. 'Units, Dimensions of', *Encyclopedia Britannica*, Cambridge: University Press, 1910-11, vol. 27, p. 737.

5. P. A. M. Dirac, Le Banquet Nobel en 1933, *Les Prix Nobel en 1933*, 1935, p. 78.

6. M. B. Lindblad, Le Banquet Nobel en 1938, *Les Prix Nobel en 1938*, 1939, p. 38.

7. John Neff, 'The Value of Diagnostic Tests: Probability Considerations in Clinical Medicine', *Diagnostic Procedures in Cardiology: A Clinician's Guide*, eds. James V. Warren and Richard P. Lewis, Chicago: Year Book Medical Publishers Inc., 1985, p. 9.

8. Claire Selltiz et al., *Research Methods in Social Relations*, Reprinted, Delhi: Surjeet Publications, 2007, p. 411.

9. 'Arithmetic', *Encyclopedia Britannica*, op. cit., vol. 2, p. 542.

10. S. P. Gupta, *Elementary Statistical Methods*, New Delhi: S. Chand and Sons, 1983, p. 148.

11. Edgar Altenburg, *Genetics*, New York: Holt, Rinehart and Winston, 1957, p. 70.

12. J. F. Kenney and E. S. Keeping, *Mathematics of Statistics*, New Jersey: D. Van Nostrand Company, Inc., 1954, vol. 1, p. 77.

13. George W. Burns, *The Science of Genetics: An Introduction to Heredity*, New York: Macmillan, 1969, p. 186.

14. J. F. Kenney and E. S. Keeping, op. cit., p. 183.

Chapter VII

MATHEMATICS AND MODELS

The word *model* in its earlier existence was confined to three-dimensional replica of anything. For a long time, even when the meaning of the term *model* was broadened, scientists used to make three-dimensional replicas. As late as the 1950s, Watson and Crick had built a three-dimensional model of the deoxyribonucleic acid. There were even models to depict economic phenomena. Even to this day, we see models of township development in remote tribal areas as shown in the exhibitions. However, in the hands of practising scientists, the word *model* took new meanings. Mathematical equations and geometric representations were used in the place of models. The atomic model of Rutherford is characterized by a positively charged nucleus orbited by a negatively charged electron either in an elliptical or circular fashion.

Scientists of an earlier generation were aware of the size effect, the fact that the actual thing might not work in the manner the model worked, owing to the increase in size. And it was a daunting task to design machines that did work in their actual form. This was another aspect of modelling.

However, the aspect of modelling that concerns us here is the mathematical representation of reality through mathematical relations or equations. Although Kirchhoff said that his aim was *description*, not *explanation*, he was led into modelling by the very *means* of description. This eventually led to mathematical phenomenology, or phenomena by analogy.[1] The mathematical modelling of elementary phenomenon and the modelling of subsequent larger groupings of the phenomena began.

The views of Maxwell on this point are noteworthy. Robert P. Crease writes that Maxwell told his students that analogies are not about *resemblances* but *relations*. It is not like reading a magazine, where we do not expect one page to throw light on the next; it is like reading a novel, where subjects introduced at the beginning reappear in complex and subtle form later. 'Thus exploring the extent to which a strange new phenomenon is like another well-known one, making adjustments where needed, can be a fruitful way to get a grip on the former.'[2]

Now let us familiarize ourselves with some simple mathematical models represented by equations following Jan Tinbergen.[3]

$$a_{11} x_1 = b_1$$
$$a_{22} x_2 = b_2$$

Here in the above equations, the unknowns are represented by x_1 and x_2, and the given quantities are indicated by a's and b's. The unknown x_1 does not appear in the second equation and, therefore, is not determined by b_2 or a_{22}. Each unknown is determined independently of the others.

$$a_{11} x_1 + a_{12} x_2 = b_1$$
$$a_{21} x_1 + a_{22} x_2 = b_2$$

Here in the above equations, the unknowns x_1 and x_2 occur in both the equations, and therefore, there is complete interdependence. 'No single can be determined independently of the others.'

One of the fundamental considerations affecting equations is linearity. Physiologists have made use of it, and economists have made use of it. In linear problems, the sum or difference of any two particular solutions is also a solution. 'If L is a linear operation and its action upon a quantity A produces the result a, whilst its operation upon B produces the result b, then the result of the operation of L upon A plus B will be a plus b.'[4]

$$\text{Let } f(x) = f_0 + x f_1 + x^2 f_2 + \ldots$$

Then if the function $f(x)$ is linear, all the other terms, except the first two, go to zero or diminish so rapidly to be of any importance.

Economic growth can be modelled through mathematics. On the vertical axis (y-axis) we use a semi-logarithmic scale such that horizontal lines are placed at logarithmic intervals. On the horizontal, or x-axis, we take time. Then, if we have data for two or more years, we can calculate the growth-rate coefficient using the following formula:[5]

$$\log \frac{x_2}{x_1} = 0.434(t_2 - t_1)k$$

Here in the above formula, x_1 and x_2 are the figures for gross domestic product for two selected years. Their ratio is taken. Then the common logarithm to the base 10 of the ratio is found out. Time is represented by t, such as 2005 and 2010. When all the variables are put into the equation, the growth rate (k) is obtained.

The use of mathematics in science begins with a numerical quantity. A numerical quantity is a number with a unit. When any arbitrary unit is specified, we can measure quantities similar to the unit. Thus, length can be measured by centimetres, and money by rupees. The specification of a unit belongs to the theory of measurement. In ordinary geometry, when we determine the area of a rectangle, we do not specify a *unit* area to determine the area of the rectangle.[6] We make use of other formulae. However, in coordinate geometry, theoretically, units can be used to measure quantities. Integral calculus is used to measure curved length. We can even, in diagrams, specify the x-axis as ordinal and the y-axis as cardinal. In fact, this is done in the case of ordinary utility measurement in elementary textbooks on microeconomics.

One of the elementary mathematical operations is rate and ratio; they are basic to almost all the sciences. A rate is expressed in the form[7]

$$\left(\frac{a}{a+b}\right)k \, .$$

Here a, the numerator, is a component part of the denominator; a can be the frequency with which an event has occurred during some specified period of time, and $a + b$ can be the number of persons exposed to the event during the same period of time. The base k is a number such as 10, 100, or 1,000 to avoid very small numbers. In sociology, urban divorce rates, marriage rates, and crime rates are the popular ones.

A ratio is of the form

$$\left(\frac{c}{d}\right)k \, .$$

Here the numerator is not a component part of the denominator; c and d are the frequency of occurrence of some event or item, and k is a base such as 1 or 100. Examples of ratios are person-doctor ratio and person-hospital-bed ratio.

References

1. 'Model', *Encyclopedia Britannica*, Cambridge: University Press, 1910-11, vol. 18, p. 640.
2. Robert P. Crease, *The Great Equations*, London: Robinson, 2009, p. 137.

3. Jan Tinbergen, *Economic Policy: Principles and Design*, Amsterdam: North-Holland Publishing Company, 1967, p. 31.

4. John D. Barrow, *Theories of Everything*, London: Vintage, 2005, p. 193.

5. Geoffrey Gordon, *System Simulation*, New Delhi: Prentice-Hall of India, 2004, pp. 85-86.

6. 'Menstruation', *Encyclopedia Britannica*, op. cit., vol. 18, pp. 134-135.

7. Wayne W. Daniel, *Biostatistics*, New York: John Wiley and Sons, Inc., 2000, pp. 737-738.

CHAPTER VIII

QUALITATIVE DATA ANALYSIS

In contrast to quantitative data analysis, which is usually based upon variables, there is qualitative analysis of data. Fields such as anthropology, medicine (nursing research), and media have made the most use of qualitative data. There are certain theories behind qualitative research such as ethnography, grounded theory, and phenomenology.

Ethnography was special to the social anthropologist who had understood the importance of assigning numbers to any phenomena but had found instead the richness of data in any thorough investigation. Instead of thinning the data over many informants, the social anthropologist saw the usefulness of *thick* description of a few informants. Techniques such as key-informant technique and the spending of prolonged periods of research in the field developed. Fieldwork was the peculiar invention of the social anthropologist since the tribes and primitive people that he studied were history-less. Fieldwork, therefore, was a substitute for history.

In fact, before the concept of qualitative research began in the social sciences including nursing, anthropologists were already doing it. In the special foreword to the third edition of his book *The Sexual Life of Savages*, Bronislaw Malinowski has extensively discussed about ethnography.[1] The fieldworker or functionalist studies any culture as a system in *equilibrium*. He does not speculate on the origin in time or diffusion in space of cultural elements such as traits. The fieldworker begins with a theory of a purely empirical nature. He studies a tribe as a self-contained reality. The culture and cultural elements of a tribe are not considered extraneous by the fieldworker. This is in contrast to the view of the diffusionist, who considers cultural elements as diffused from other areas, and the evolutionist, who considers it as a survival of the past.

A careful reading of the paragraphs would suggest that Malinowski was critical of both the evolutionist and the diffusionist schools and their method of research—the comparative method. The comparative method, which was proud of its *unhistorical* nature and would compare trait for trait without the context, is here criticized by Malinowski. But in this criticism, Malinowski is led to argue for the qualitative method.

Phenomenology studies the 'meaning, truth, and reality' of a phenomenon from the lived experience of subjects. Grounded theory is another qualitative approach in which data collection and analysis are concurrent and ongoing, with more specific data collected based on the analysis of initial data.[2]

Our point is that ethnographers such as Malinowski had already laid the foundation of the concepts needed for qualitative research such as the role of the *context*, the *meaning* of their lives to the people, and the completion of research in the field (grounded theory).

Qualitative data does not need any elaborate sampling procedures such as simple random sampling or stratified random sampling. The data required for the purpose should be *appropriate*. It is appropriate in the sense that the informant is able to convey the necessary information to the interviewer. When, for example, the anthropologist selects the medicine man as the informant, he has, at the back of his mind, the feeling that the medicine man and not any ordinary man can furnish the specialized information. Secondly, the data ought to be *adequate*. There is a rule of thumb in social anthropology that a sample size of 250 is adequate much as the experimental geneticist considers 400 as an adequate sample size.

Qualitative data tries to understand what is going on in any particular situation rather than counting the number of heads present.

Qualitative data is not new to science such as biology. Much before the anthropologist made use of it, Charles Darwin had made use of it in his studies.

Some of the outstanding accomplishments of biologic science—including the work of Darwin, Virchow, and modern geneticists and electron microscopists—have been based on precise, reproducible, but non-dimensional descriptions. With better standards of observation and classification, the verbal categories of 'soft' clinical data could readily be improved into 'hard' scientific quality.[3]

Again, we are being led to the conviction that it is the *reproducibility* of data that matters to science, both qualitative and quantitative. Many of our natural scientists and social scientists have spoken of understanding, and we do not mean to wish to demean the importance of understanding in social science. A lawyer, for example, ought to understand the case of his client before he suggests remedies— remedies that are general and applicable to any specific case. And since in qualitative research we have underlined the importance of meaning, of lived experience, we ought to find a place for understanding and not only for regularity or frequency. When the French anthropologist Claude Lévi-Strauss vouched for the context-free analysis of language, he was well aware of the fact that language operates at the level of the unconscious. Anthropologists are still discussing whether to study culture as context-driven as Malinowski did or whether to follow Leslie White and study the mutual relationships of cultural elements to each other while the human actor is sent to the background. We believe that any new developments in the field of qualitative research ought to come from the students of man and his culture, the anthropologists. The recent idea at *triangulation*, or the combination of quantitative with the qualitative approach, is promising.

References

1. Bronislaw Malinowski, *The Sexual Life of Savages*, Calcutta: The Standard Literature, 1952, pp. xxix-xxxii.
2. J. R. Hott and W. C. Budin, *Notter's Essentials of Nursing Research*, New York: Springer, 2006, p. 35.
3. Alvan R. Feinstein, 'Science, Clinical Medicine, and the Spectrum of disease', *Textbook of Medicine*, eds. Beeson-Mcdermott, Philadelphia: Saunders, 1975, p. 3.

Chapter IX

RESEARCH PROTOCOL

A personal communication[1] to one of the authors suggested the following outline for a research project.

1. Statement of the Problem
    a. Importance of the study
    b. Review of the literature
    c. Gaps in the existing studies
    d. Select some gaps in the existing studies
2. Objectives of the Study
3. Hypotheses (if you want to test any)
4. Methodology
    a. Sources of data and information
    b. Data recasting
    c. Data processing
5. Limitations of the Study
6. Layout of the Study

It was suggested by another professor that a scholar ought to read three to four books before embarking upon research. Quite often, it is reported that the researcher went to the field, having in his kit one or two books on research methodology. Time is always insufficient for the researcher. It had been reported in the past that *Encyclopedia Britannica* used to give a time of one year to the writer of a long article. Since time is always scarce and other demanding tasks have always a stake in time, it is clear that the researcher does not work to the full efficiency. Since time is scarce and could always be devoted to some other cunning business to earn money, a Nobel laureate laughingly remarked on the television on why he gave so much time to the writing of books.

The importance of the study is mentioned so that the consumer of the research or the funding agency is willing to fund the project. With the mining industry gaining an upper hand in the exploitation of the natural resources and the consequent displacement of tribal people from their native lands, many researchers tried to do impact studies. In economics and sociology, the impact of globalization on the native economy and culture is a leading issue. But in tackling these problems, the researcher often, if he is an individual researcher, limits the scope of his studies to a limited area or a limited group. Environmental pollution in a particular area or the working of the midday-meal programme in schools in a particular locality often turn out to be good research proposals. In this age of electronic communication, when the media does the initial research in many areas that catches the imagination, such research is often followed up by other serious researchers. Invitees to media discussions, in spite of their technical competence in their respective areas, are asked to give their opinions in an environment of conversation with the host in plain English, and the viewer is at his discretion whether such conversation enlightened him or not.

Often the topic of research is suggested by the funding agency, whether the funding agency is external or internal headed by the director of an institute. Here the wide experience of the director and other senior scientists often prove to be of benefit to the research scholar in identifying the topic. The research scholar is asked to prepare a review of the literature and, if possible, a schedule to fill the data later. Visits to different libraries in the city, photocopying relevant materials from both new and old journals, and surfing the Net provide the initial stage for research.

Acquaintance with theory is a prerequisite to conducting successful research and in identifying the problem, although often theory such as economic theory is distinguished from economic problems. Robert Andrews Millikan said forcefully on this point:

> The fact that science walks forward on two feet, namely theory and experiment, is nowhere better illustrated than in the two fields for slight contributions to which you have done me the great honour of awarding me the Nobel prize in Physics for the year 1923.

> Sometimes it is one foot which is put forward first, sometimes the other, but continuous progress is only made by the use of both—by theorizing and then

testing, or by finding new relations in the process of experimenting and then bringing the theoretical foot up and pushing it on beyond, and so on in unending alteration.[2]

The central message of Millikan is that the identification of a problem does lead to the identification of newer problems when experiments are undertaken. In social science, the data collected in surveys may suggest new hypotheses and may alter the character of the conclusions.

Once the problem has been identified, the researcher goes on to review the literature on the subject. On the occasion of the Nobel Prize in Physiology or Medicine for 1933, Folke Henschen reviewed the findings of Mendelian genetics in the following manner:

Mendel's observations are of revolutionizing importance. As a matter of fact they completely upset the older theories of heredity, although this was not at all appreciated by his contemporaries. Mendel's discoveries usually are stated in two heredity laws or better rules of heredity. The first of his rules, the cleaving rule, means that of two different hereditary dispositions or hereditary factors, *genes*, for a certain quality—for instance for size—are combined in one generation, they separate in the following generation. If, for instance, a constantly tall race is crossed with a constantly short race, the individuals of next generation become altogether medium-sized, or, if the factor tall is dominant, exclusively tall. In the following generation, however, a cleaving takes place, so that once more the size of the individuals becomes variable according to certain numerical proportions, then of four descendants, one tall, two medium-sized, and one short.

The second of Mendel's rules, the rule of free combinations, means that, when new generations arise, the different hereditary factors can form new combinations independent of each other. If, for instance, a tall, red-flowered plant is crossed with a short, white-flowered one, the factors red and white can be inherited independent of the factors large and small. The second generation then, besides tall red-flowered and short white-flowered plants, produces short red-flowered and tall white-flowered ones.[3]

We see in the above paragraphs that the writer has been able to digest what Mendel had proved in his experiments and is able to communicate the matter both to the professional colleague and the general reader. In fact, the above paragraphs are the succinct exposition of Mendel's contribution to heredity. We had said in an earlier paragraph that the researcher ought to familiarize himself with the theories in his field of research so that he does not only *describe* the data but *explain* it through simpler concepts. Mendel not only described his experiments; he explained it through arithmetic, and in the process, quantitative genetics took its birth.

By the time Thomas Hunt Morgan began his studies, Mendel's laws had been extended to other plants and animals, and there were even cases of exceptions to the laws. Morgan's studies and experiments led to the discovery of *additional* laws and, thereby, filled the gaps in the path of knowledge. In the words of Morgan, 'We now know that some of these exceptions [to Mendel's laws] are due to newly discovered and demonstrable properties of the chromosome mechanism, and others to recognizable irregularities in the machine.'[4]

Objectives of any study can be theoretical or the discovery of new observations. Heisenberg had won the Nobel Prize for theoretical physics while Chadwick won it two years later for the discovery of neutron. In ordinary research, the objectives are always led to fruition by tests such as a test of significance or the establishment of a relationship through correlation. The research usually begins with the statement 'To determine . . .'. However, for the purpose of science, it is required that the objectives are made operational or measurable. The counting of frequency or regularity is usually the least that can be done while there are other advanced tools. The social anthropologist who believes in qualitative research usually does not attempt to measure anything. He is more interested in knowing what is going on in any particular situation than counting the number of heads present. In economics, the objective might be the determination of household consumption expenditure, and for that purpose, the whole of a country can be the candidate. Here the objective cannot be divorced from the plan of sampling to be done to collect the data. There are agricultural censuses as well as urban studies, and some of them can be of enormous size. Commissions in India, such as the

National Commission on Agriculture, have in the past produced valuable and everlasting pieces of reference for the research scholar. The individual researcher, on the other hand, has a limited set of objectives. The demand for fish in Bhubaneswar, for example, is a limited objective, but to make it successful, the researcher might have to rely on sampling techniques adopted in countrywide surveys such as stratification and selected random sample.

When Francis Bacon was alive, the foundations of the inductive method were laid. Scientists who employed induction by enumeration, or the Baconian induction by elimination, began their career. At this time, practising scientists felt the need for hypotheses to organize their data. The mere collection of data without any hypothesis to guide it was felt to be insufficient. In the practice of research, it has been found that the scientist formulates a hypothesis, tests it against evidence, and if the evidence does not support the hypothesis, reformulates it. Sometimes the hypothesis leads to fruition such as what happened when the wobbling of the planet Uranus led to the discovery of Neptune.

In ordinary research, the scientist might formulate the hypothesis that 'the coin is fair'. How does he test the hypothesis? If the coin is fair, it should show heads as many times as it should show tails. The probability of a head or a tail is ½ or 0.5. There is a convention in statistics that suggests that the probability of the coin showing heads consecutively twenty times is 0.5 multiplied by itself twenty times. The probability is miniscule. In fact, if you multiply 0.5 by itself five times with the help of an ordinary calculator, the result would be zero. Therefore, since the probability of a coin showing heads consecutively in twenty throws is miniscule, any coin that does so is loaded; it is unfair.

Data can be either primary or secondary. Data collected from the field by the investigator himself or by his men are primary. These are the original data. Data collected from handbooks and other published sources are secondary. The primary data is often furnished by the village watchman, and thereby, the accuracy of the data or its deviation from the true value remains dubious. Sometimes, the informant furnishes inaccurate data owing to forgetfulness. While the economist spends his time in the village panchayat or office block collecting his data, the social anthropologist spends his time collecting data from the family. He can even *code* the data by the frequency of utterance of a particular word or concept by the informants. The nature of data is its flow. The individual researcher often draws on the data furnished by world bodies while the primary data collected from the field finds its way upward and is incorporated in worldwide publications.

In economics, data collected and then tabulated at the unit level is transformed to the group level, and this is termed *recasting*.

Any study has its own limitations. Sometimes the limitation is set by the level of technique available at the disposal of the investigator. There are periods in the year when data cannot be collected. Sometimes, for the purpose of convenience, residents of the ground floor are contacted to the exclusion of other residents. Sometimes when the modal class of any specific characteristic is contacted to the exclusion of other groups, the variability of the data is affected. The data becomes homogeneous. In experiments, sometimes the size of the sample turns out to be less than ten, and the prevalence of such circumstances in the past led to the theory of small samples such the *t*-test.

References

1. Personal note given to one of the authors by former professor of economics of Utkal University, A. K. Mitra.
2. Robert Andrews Millikan, 'The Electron and the Light-quant from the Experimental Point of View', *Les Prix Nobel en 1923*, 1924, p. 1.
3. Folke Henschen, The Nobel Prize in Physiology and Medicine for the year 1933, *Les Prix Nobel en 1933*, 1935, p. 56.
4. Thomas Hunt Morgan, 'The Relation of Genetics to Physiology and Medicine', *Les Prix Nobel en 1933*, 1935, p. 2.

CHAPTER X

WRITING RESEARCH REPORT

The first requirement of a good research report is the use of correct English. The research scholar is usually required in the beginning to prepare a bibliography. To prepare a bibliography on any particular topic, the research scholar should, in the beginning, consult an encyclopedia or handbook. There are both general encyclopedias and special encyclopedias. Most of the libraries in a big city have copies of a general encyclopedia, such as the *Encyclopedia Britannica*. There are several editions of this encyclopedia, and the reader should consult the edition that is available in the library. Encyclopedia articles themselves are based upon books, and at the end of each major article, a list of books is appended. Recent editions of the encyclopedia are based upon the earlier editions as well as on encyclopedias published in the other major languages of the world besides English.

Since encyclopedias are based upon books, they are referred to as the tertiary sources of reference. The primary source is a research article in a journal; the secondary source is a book. The reason behind consulting an encyclopedia is to consult subsequently the books listed at the end of a long article. The range of the books varies. Sometimes there is the mention of original books by a famous author, but in addition to that, there are also standard reference books including textbooks. Following a top-down approach, the scholar begins to consult the books. In every such book at the end of each chapter or at the end of the book, he is likely to find the list of journal articles upon which the chapters of the book are based.

Some experts advise that a research scholar ought to consult an author in the original and should not rely upon commentaries. This advice is not always workable. Sometimes the original author is hard to understand, and at other times, he is unavailable. In that case, encyclopedias and commentaries on the original author ought to be consulted. But it is easy to find an article of an original author in a reputed journal, and most of the university libraries have a journal section in which such journals are available. Parija Library of Utkal University (Bhubaneswar) has stocks of journals in many subjects, dating back to the beginning of the twentieth century, and the Odisha State Archives has records dating back to 1803, the time when Odisha came under the British rule.

The purpose behind preparing a bibliography or reference list is to familiarize the scholar with the preparation of cards that later prove to be of help in writing the report. Some even argue to the extent that once the cards are put into place, it is only secondary to write the report following the cards. The cards are of different types such as a keyword card or a bibliography card.

While it was an earlier practice to prepare cards before research begins, nowadays it is possible for the research scholar to write directly with the help of a computer. Editing on a computer is easy. Once a rough draft is ready, it is a less hard task than it used to be before to sift other relevant materials into the text. And the essence of research is *sifting* to give the thesis a new form. With direct quotations and the rewording of quotations in the language of the scholar, the research worker should be able to organize his original findings with the general body of truths of his subject. Many a times, it is the verdict of history that the original research of a scholar is the extension of what was known already. When Student developed his theory of small samples, or the *t*-test, and gave us a new probability curve, it was found to be superior in contrast to the classical probability theory, but the concepts of the *t*-test themselves were based upon the classical theory. At other times, it is the verdict of history that the method of one field of science was successfully applied to another field. Whether it is the application of phonetics and phonemics to the study of culture or the application of thermodynamic principles to economics, the result was new insight. This does not mean that there is no conflict. Sometimes concepts have been applied out of context and, therefore, have been criticized. Nobody knows for sure whether the economy as a whole (macroeconomics) is to be understood as a mechanical whole or an organic whole. If it is a mechanical whole, its functioning ought to be explained in terms of matter and motion; if it is an organic whole, its functioning ought to be understood in terms of growth, senility, and decay. In point of fact, the analogy of an organism is strong in a field such as the arts, sculptural and otherwise.

We have said that mastery of functional English is essential for a good research worker. When taking notes, for example, the scholar is required to turn a complex or compound or a long simple sentence into a short simple sentence. Thus, the sentence 'The sick man drinks pure water copiously' can be reduced to 'Man drinks'. All the eliminated words are not essential to the sentence. In fact, by the elimination of several inessential words, we have turned a particular sentence into a general one.

'Style is the man' goes an old saying. The essence of the sentence is that among all animals, only man has a distinctive style. Every man is different from the other while the roar of any lion is indistinguishable from any other lion. Even if the style of every man is different, the scholar ought to learn from the masters of style.

> The authority of such men as Shakespeare, Addison, Dryden, is, in grammar, paramount and supreme. What they do we must follow, and we must follow it because it is their practice. Their words, their forms of speech, their constructions must be ours. They are our masters, we their scholars. They give laws, we obey the laws they give.[2]

Style is essential for those readers who look for pleasure, not mere information. Bald statements are no substitute for imaginative writing. Style in writing can cause a heightened pulse.[3]

However, the same article goes on to say that 'before there can be style, therefore, there must be thought, clearness of knowledge, precise experience, sanity of reasoning power'. [4]

Style appeals to a man of experience. 'The deep delight with which a grown man of experience reads Milton or Dante is but the same phenomenon produced in different conditions.'[5]

Style is specific to a particular age. 'That kind of writing which in its own age is extravagantly cultivated and admired may, in the next age, be as violently repudiated; this does not preclude the possibility of its recovering critical if not popular favour.'[6]

Anyone who reads a lecture printed in *Les Prix Nobel* would not fail to notice how the scientist has measured his words. In the space of a few pages, he has been able to cover all the aspects of scientific writing including the technical requirements of statement of the problem, review of the literature, technique of experiment, and the findings. The scientist has, at his disposal, a simple problem. Consider the following observations of Professor Waller on the occasion of the 1949 Nobel Prize in Physics:

> Attacking the problem of the nature of the nuclear forces, Yukawa used the electromagnetic field as a model. He found that this field could be modified so as to give forces which like the nuclear forces have a short range. He therefore assumed that the new field

corresponds to the nuclear forces. Each field of force is, according to modern theories, associated with some kind of particle. Yukawa discovered that there is a simple relation between the range of the forces and the mass of the corresponding particles.[7]

In essence, the modern rules of style suggest that the writer should choose words that are direct, familiar, and concrete.

Along with the preliminaries of research, the scientist ought to familiarize himself on how to quote the writings of others. The rules of quotation as followed in the eleventh edition of the *Encyclopedia Britannica* correspond to that given by Brenda Spatt in the book *Writing from Sources*. The rules are:[8]

1. All full stops and commas are placed inside the terminal quotation marks whether they belong to the original sentence or not.

2. All semicolons, colons, and dashes are placed outside the terminal quotation marks, regarded as the punctuation marks of the present writer.

3. Question marks and exclamation points are sometimes placed inside the quotation marks and sometimes placed outside. When the quotation is a question or exclamation, the quotation mark goes inside; when the quotation mark is the writer's, it is placed outside.

The next thing that troubles the writer is the use of figures. Here the practice varies. One recommendation is to use the numeral for technical units of measurement and for experimental data. Other than that, one or two-word numbers should be spelt out.[9]

F. Howard Collins recommends figures for ages, dates, degrees, distances, dollars, scores, specific gravity, statistics, times of day, votes, and weights. He recommends figures spelt out for beginning of sentences, indefinite amounts, and legal work.[10]

There are other areas in English such as the agreement of tenses and the agreement of parts of speech that might create problems for the student. While it is correct to say, 'He *thinks* he *can* . . .' it is desirable to say, 'He *thought* he *could* . . .' There are one or two exceptions to this rule. 'He said that the sun *rises* in the east' is grammatically correct since the truth is universal. Similarly, 'The message said that thousands *are* starving' is correct when the condition still exists.[11]

There are books that suggest using verbs in the place of nouns. For example, it is advised to use 'add x and y' in the place of 'the addition of x and y'.

References

1. 'English', *The New Popular Educator*, London: Cassell and Company, Limited, no date, vol. 5, p. 179.
2. Ibid. vol. 1, p. 2.
3. 'Style', *The Encyclopedia Britannica*, Cambridge: University Press, 1910-11, p. 1056.
4. Ibid.
5. Ibid.
6. Ibid. p. 1058.
7. I. Waller, The 1949 Nobel Prize for Physics, *Les Prix Nobel en 1949*, 1950, p. 21.
8. Brenda Spatt, *Writing from Sources*, New York: St. Martin's Press, 1996, pp. 96-97.

9. Joseph Gibaldi, *MLA Handbook for Writers of Research Papers*, New York: The Modern Language Association of America, 1995, p. 61.

10. F. Howard Collins, *Authors' and Printers' Dictionary*, London: Oxford University Press1944, pp. 121-122.

11. Lois Hutchinson, *Standard Handbook for Secretaries*, New York: McGraw-Hill Book Company, Inc., 1964, p. 92.

APPENDIX I

The following extracts are taken from the introduction to *The History, Antiquities, Topography, and Statistics of Eastern India* by Montgomery Martin, London, 1838, as republished in *Why Statistics and Other Essays* of P. C. Mahalanobis, edited by P. K. Bose and published by Statistical Publishing Society, Calcutta, pp. 64-67.

'Your inquiries are to extend throughout the whole of the territories subject to the immediate authority of the Presidency of Fort William.

'The Governor General in Council is of opinion that these inquiries should commence in the district of Rungpur, and that from thence you should proceed to the west-ward through each district on the north side of the ganges, until you reach the western boundary of the Honourable Company's provinces. You will then proceed towards the south and east, until you have examined all the districts on the south side of the great river, and afterwards proceed of Dacca, and the other districts towards the eastern frontier.

'Your inquiries should be particularly directed to the following subjects, which you are to examine with as much accuracy as local circumstances will admit.

'I.   A Topographical account of district, including the extent, soil, plains, mountains, rivers, harbours, towns, and subdivisions; together with an account of the air and weather, and whatever you may discover worthy of remark concerning the history and antiquities of the country.

'II.   The condition of the Inhabitants; their number, the state of their food, clothing and habitations; the peculiar diseases to which they are liable; together with the means that have been taken or may be proposed to remove them; the education of youth; and the provision or resources for the indigent.

'III.   Religion; the number, progress and most remarkable customs of each different sect or tribe of which the population consists; together with the emoluments and power which their priests and chiefs enjoy; and what circumstances exist or may probably arise that might attach them to Government, or render them disaffected.

'IV.   The Natural Productions of the Country, animal, vegetable, and mineral; especially such as are made use in diet, in medicine, in commerce, or in arts and manufactures. The following works deserve your particular attention:

'1st.   The fisheries, their extent, the manner in which they are conducted, and the obstacles that appear to exist against their improvement and extension.

'2nd. The forests, of which you will endeavour to ascertain the extent and situation, with respect to water conveyance. You will investigate the kind of trees which they contain, together with their comparative value and you will, point out such means, as occur to you, for increasing the number of the more valuable kinds, or for introducing new ones that may be still more useful.

'3rd. The mine and quarries are objects of particular concern. You will investigate their produce, the manner of working them, and the state of the people employed.

'V. Agriculture, under which head your inquiries are to be directed to the following points:

'1st. The different kinds of vegetables cultivated, whether for food, forage, medicine, or intoxication, or as raw materials for the arts: the modes of cultivation adopted for each kind; the seasons when they are sown and reaped; the value of the produce of a given extent of land cultivated with each kind. The profit arising to the cultivator from each, and the manner in which each is prepared and fitted for the market. Should it appear that any new object of cultivation could be introduced with advantage you will suggest the means by which its introduction may be encouraged.

'2nd. The implements of husbandry employed with the defects and advantages of each and suggestions for the introduction of new ones, that may be more effectual.

'3rd. The manure employed for the soil, especially the means used for irrigation.

'4th. The means used for excluding floods and inundations, with such remarks as may occur to you on the defects in their management.

'5th. The different breeds of the cattle, poultry, and other domestic animals reared by the natives. The manner in which they are bred and kept; the profits derived from rearing and maintaining them; the kinds used in labour; whether the produce of the country be sufficient, without importation, to answer the demand, or to enable the farmer to export; and whether any kinds not now reared might be advantageously introduced.

'6th. Fences the various kinds that are used, and the might be introduced, with observations concerning the utility of this part of agriculture in the present state of the country.

'7th. The state of farms; their usual size, the stock required, with the manner in which it is procured; the expense of management the rent, whether paid in specie or in kind; the wages and condition of farming servants and labourers employed in husbandry; tenures by which farms are held, with their comparative advantages, and the means which, in your opinion, may be employed to extend and improve the cultivation of the country.

'8th. The state of the landed property and of the tenures by which it is held in so far as these seem to affect agriculture.

'VI. The progress made by the natives in the fine arts in the common arts and the state of the manufactures; you will describe their architecture sculpture and paintings and inquire into the different processes and machinery used by their workmen and procure an account of the various kinds and amount of goods manufactured in each district. It should also be an object of your attention to ascertain the ability of the country to produce the raw materials used in them; and what proportion, if any is necessary to be imported from other countries and under what advantages or disadvantages such importation now is, or might be made; you will also ascertain how the necessary capital is procured, the situation of the artists and manufactures, the mode of providing their goods the usual rates of their labour; any particular advantages they may enjoy, their comparative affluence with respect to the cultivators of the land, their domestic usages, the nature of their sales, and the regulations respecting their markets. Should it appear to you that any new art or manufacture might be introduced with advantage into any district, you are to point out in what manner you think it may be accomplished.

'VII. Commerce; the quantity of goods exported and imported in each district the manner of conducting sales, especially at fairs and markets; the regulation of money, weights, and measures; the nature of the conveyance of goods by land and water and the means by which this may be facilitated, especially by making or repairing roads.

'In addition to the foregoing objects of inquiry, you will take opportunity of forwarding to the Company's Botanical Garden at this presidency, whatever useful or rare and curious plants and seeds you may be enabled to acquire in the progress of your researches with such observations as may be necessary for their culture.'

INDEX

A

D

E

N

O

P

Q

R

S

T

U

V

W

Y

Z